Angels and Demons
The Truth Behind the Encounters

David Lamb

Marshall Pickering
An Imprint of HarperCollins*Publishers*

Marshall Pickering is an Imprint of
HarperCollins*Religious*
Part of HarperCollins*Publishers*
77–85 Fulham Palace Road, London W6 8JB

First published in Great Britain in 1999 by Marshall Pickering

1 3 5 7 9 10 8 6 4 2

David Lamb asserts the moral right to be identified as the author of this work

A catalogue record for this book is available from the British Library

ISBN 0 551 03221 9

Printed and bound in Great Britain by
Caledonian International Book Manufacturing Ltd, Glasgow

Contents

Acknowledgements

Writing a book is hard work, and much help has been received from friends to enable this one to be completed.

The author would like to thank:

Rebecca Reveley for transcribing the sermon tapes
Rita Maria Fletcher and Robert Clement for many hours spent typing the manuscript and stories
Donald Banks for his hard work in editing the book

A special thank-you goes to Beverley Clement for long hours of typing, editing and writing stories, sometimes until the early hours of the morning.

The author is very grateful to all those who have contributed stories, whether or not they appear in the book.

Finally, for all the intercessors who have prayed this book into being, there are eternal rewards from God.

Foreword

The whole subject of angels and demons is difficult. There are so many things about the supernatural that we find difficult to understand with our natural minds.

One thing is clear from the Bible: both angels and demons definitely exist. Angels ministered to Jesus and he cast demons out of people. He taught about both, and it is clear from the book of Revelation that angels have a major role to play in God's end-time purposes. In this book, David Lamb speaks clearly from the biblical understanding of these supernatural beings. Whatever we read in the scriptures is to be fully trusted.

In seeking to understand the meaning and significance of angels and demons, it is almost inevitable that we move into speculation. This becomes obvious when people recount their experiences, in which it seems clear that only intervention from angelic beings could have saved them from disaster. I can sympathize with them, as I have known a number of such occurrences in my own experience. The problem is that it is almost impossible to prove to anyone that angels were ministering to you.

Much debate rages in Christian circles about terrestrial spirits and whether we as Christians need to be involved in spiritual warfare with these beings. There is further disagreement as to how this warfare should be conducted.

David Lamb is brave in writing this book, but he is a man of real and bold faith. Perhaps you will not agree with everything he says. Perhaps you will find some things beyond credulity. Perhaps you would put a different interpretation on certain events described.

Nevertheless, this book will help you in some significant ways. It is thought-provoking and in some ways challenging. It will certainly increase your understanding of the biblical teaching on angels and demons. Above all, it will help you to see that God has a vast army of angelic servants he uses to minister to or to serve his children. And you will be reminded of the authority God has given you over all the works of the evil one.

It is not for us to evoke angels, command angels or to seek angelic visitations. To do these things opens the door to deception. God commands his angels, and he is willing to deploy them for your good!

Colin Urquhart

Introduction

Imagine an advert: *Wanted, for the post of an angel* ... Have you considered their job description? Superman and Superwoman do not start to compare. The angels of God have a multi-faceted job. They make the choice either to be seen, as angels or humankind, or to remain invisible. They travel at incredible speeds throughout heaven, the galaxies, earth and even hell.

They have authority over territories and countries, people and demons, and have access to a vast array of weaponry – bolts of lightning, thunder, earthquakes and flaming swords. Their great strength was demonstrated by Michael, the archangel, when he evicted Lucifer from heaven. They are constantly attacking and defeating hordes of dark spirits and demonic armies – there are no days off in the war in the cosmos. Although they are indestructible, the battle is real, and it seems they can be wounded and need restoration. The rewards for their diligence are the heirs of salvation.

Different shifts enable the angels to worship before the throne of God. Here on earth, angels attend those in distress and in life-threatening situations. Wounded soldiers have reportedly been carried by angels to safety, aeroplane and ship disasters have been averted by them, children and babies are protected by them, and some children have reported seeing them. Their main job, however, is to deliver the heirs of salvation from harm.

In the Bible they are messengers bringing prophetic words and revealing the birth of Christ with great joy and glory. They rescued Lot and torched Sodom and Gomorrah to the ground. King Herod and thousands upon thousands of Assyrian soldiers were killed by them. In this age they set up divine appointments bringing visions, dreams and instruction. They are responsible for gathering in the great harvest of those who come to salvation in Christ. They cannot preach or lead a lost sinner to Christ, yet they party every time a sinner repents and gets right with God.

Seven mighty angels will blow the trumpet of God's judgement. One-third of the earth's rivers will be polluted, one-third of the sun, stars and moon will be destroyed. There will be great darkness. One-third of the sea will be turned to blood and one-third of the ships will be destroyed.

At the end of time angels will gather the heirs of salvation from the four corners of the earth, and bring them to Christ. They will ride behind the Messiah on His triumphant return to the earth. Judgements are given into their capable hands; humankind will be separated by them, some for eternal life and others for eternal judgements. They have the power to cast into hell.

It was an angel, not God, who cast out Lucifer from heaven, and angels will lock up Satan for a thousand years and finally send him into the lake of fire, where he will be tormented day and night for ever.

Angelic Activities in the Life of Christ

- in His birth
- in His temptation
- in His life
- in His arrest
- in His death
- in His resurrection

- in His ascension
- in His return

Other Angelic Activities

- in judgement
- in worship
- in conveying messages
- in foretelling the future
- in dreams
- in instructions
- in reaping the Great Harvest
- in travel with Jesus Christ on His return
- in warfare
- against demons
- in watching over babies

In this book we shall look in more detail and answer many questions about the activities of angels, and about the forces of evil arrayed against the heirs of salvation and how to overcome them. Angels are God's helpers, enabling us to live victoriously. I am glad to be on the Lord's side, with the angels on my side, because God always wins and there is nothing like winning.

For some readers the contents of this book may seem radical. However, many of us do not live out the full inheritance that belongs to us through Christ Jesus. The author's purpose is not to cause feelings of condemnation, but to encourage and challenge us to live more and more in the truth of who we are and what we have been given by Jesus. As you continue to read, be open to hear the voice of God through these pages.

1 God's Secret Service

Revelation of Angels

Our family business makes furniture for hotels, restaurants and churches. One day, as I was working in the office, a man came rushing in, shouting, 'The foam store is on fire!' I dialled 999 for the fire brigade. Vital minutes were lost as I had to spell my name, but finally someone from the control room answered.

'My foam store is on fire!' I said, 'Get somebody here quickly!'

I ran from my office, realizing to my horror the terrible mistake that we had made. In the area where we had stored the foam we had also stored the gas bottles used by the forklift trucks.

As I looked through the doorway across the small courtyard to the foam store, one of the gas bottles exploded, and in the brilliant light I saw the outline of a figure, standing right in front of me. I turned and ran. When I reached safety outside the building, where all the workmen were standing, I asked, 'Who was in there with me?'

They answered, 'It wasn't one of us. We got out safely as soon as the fire started.'

When the fire brigade had put the fire out, I picked my way through the debris. The foam store and half the factory had been destroyed. Between where I had been standing and the place of the explosion was a closed door, through which a piece of wood was sticking. If the door had not been closed by the mysterious figure, I would have been killed by that piece of wood. This all happened about sixteen years ago, before the dangers of foam were really understood. I know that God sent an angel to protect me and to shut the door, and that it was an angel I saw.

Trevor Bendrium; Halifax, Yorkshire

The Bible is brimming with stories and revelation of angels. History has been changed by the presence of angels, the present is alive with them, and the future will throb with supernatural interventions. Why, then, do we in the West know so little about God's secret agents? Is it because we are taught to question or discount the miraculous realm, and scepticism, rationalism and unbelief have been drilled into us from an early age?

Although few people believe that God's angels exist, more and more are being drawn towards having supernatural experiences, and are getting involved in the demonic realm by studying the occult, reading horoscopes and even practising Satanism. Yet whenever I travel to Africa or South-East Asia, supernatural events are common and expected. In these continents, where you can see the hold of Satan and the demonic realm on the lives of people, you can also see the power of God being released through God's angels.

We in the West need a fresh revelation about God's angels. I want to awaken a deep hunger in your life to know more about angels. Start to study the scriptures for yourself on this vast topic. Talk to God about angels. Ask Him to show you their ministry and how you can be involved with them in your ministry, family and workplace. We live in dangerous times: having a fresh revelation of angels and knowing their purpose and function will enable us to co-operate with them, and we shall see God's will and purpose fulfilled on the earth.

'My people are destroyed from lack of knowledge' (Hosea 4:6). We are always in need of knowledge, and must live in a continual awareness of God's almighty protection. We cannot take it for granted; we have to understand and believe that the angelic army is constantly at work.

The Glory of Angels

'For by him all things were created: things in heaven and on earth, visible and invisible, whether thrones or powers or rulers or authorities; all things were created by him and for him. He is before all things, and in him all things hold together' (Colossians 1: 16–17). God has always existed. God is the creator of all things, so He created the angels. When we compare angels to the strength, holiness and awesomeness of God, angels are a mere shadow. Yet angels are holy, awesome, mighty, beautiful beings who can talk, sing, shout and play musical instruments. In Malaysia, a group I was leading was singing and praising the Lord – and the angels joined in. That was quite an experience! On the day of judgement the angels will be blowing trumpets.

Another person to hear angels singing was Cathy Holder:

> 'My mother had just died of cancer, my teenage children were a handful, my job had gone haywire and everything seemed black,' she recalls, looking back to five years ago. After another harrowing day at work, she got into her car to make the journey home, put a worship tape on automatically and started to drive. On this occasion the noise seem to be too much and she cried out, 'I can't be bothered!' switching the tape off. Immediately the car was full of the most wonderful heavenly music and angels praising the Lord. Cathy says, 'I felt encompassed in a cloud – this is the only way I can describe what was happening. I don't remember the drive home. I knew I had been ministered to by angels. Their praising the Lord lifted me to a height I had never before experienced.'

'There are also heavenly bodies and there are earthly bodies; but the splendour of the heavenly bodies is one kind, and the splendour of the earthly bodies is another' (1 Corinthians 15:40).

When I saw an angel he appeared like a man, but angels are not human beings; they never have been and they never will be. God created them to be different and of another order. The angels that are ministering to us do not know or understand salvation. 'It was revealed to them that they were not serving themselves but you, when they spoke of the things that have now been told you by those who have preached the gospel to you by the Holy Spirit sent from heaven. Even angels long to look into these things' (1 Peter 1:12).

These holy, awesome, majestic beings, when they minister to us sinful, wayward humans, stand amazed at the grace of God. They are amazed that God could be so merciful and gracious to us unholy beings as to redeem and bring us back to Himself. Because they do not know it as we do, angels will always marvel at the grace of God.

Innumerable Angels

The empire of angels is as vast as God's creation. Impossible as it is to number the grains of sand on the seashore, so it is with the angels. Even though one-third fell from heaven to earth when Lucifer rebelled, the remainder, who are God's messengers, are innumerable.

Angels do not marry, procreate or have sex, and are created by God to do His will. They are to serve God in heaven and also release His will on earth. 'Are not all angels ministering spirits sent to serve those who will inherit salvation?' (Hebrews 1:14). As heirs of salvation we are placed in Christ and now live in heavenly places. We have forgiveness of sins, the healing of our physical bodies and deliverance from demons, and Jesus is our deliverer. He sends us His angels to save and deliver us. As soon as we cry out to God, He sends His angels to assist us.

Daniel was fasting and praying. An angel came flying through the mid-heavens to bring a message from God to him. 'Do not be afraid, Daniel. Since the first day that you set your mind to gain understanding and to humble yourself before your God, your words were heard, and I have come in response to them' (Daniel 10: 12). Colin Urquhart once said God answers prayer either like a rocket, with an instant answer, or like a tortoise, when the answer comes slowly. We may be waiting for an answer but we have to keep our faith strong, believing God will always answer.

As the climactic conclusion of God's kingdom unfolds and we are witnessing the birth pangs of Christ's return, it is imperative to understand the role angels will fulfil. We can survive the demise and shaking of the nations, thereby entering into the Church's finest hour when our Messiah will return in majestic glory with the hosts of angels. I believe the past struggles to win the lost will give way to the greatest revival ever witnessed by humankind. Angels will gather, with us, the largest, most miraculous harvest of souls ever reaped. Watch this space!

A move of God is about to break loose on the earth in an unprecedented manner. Fasten your seat belt! As the Church moves out with greater boldness into darker and darker places, angels will precede and protect us.

If you have not yet seen an angel, that does not make you a second-class citizen. 'Blessed are those who have not seen and yet have believed' (John 20:29). If you have seen an angel, it is because you needed to see one. God knows what we need. Therefore, if you have not seen one it means you have not needed to see one. When you need to see an angel, you will – God will make sure of that.

God's Warriors

Whenever I take a group out to witness, I tell them that although we may seem a small number, I tell them that although we may seem a small number, this is not the truth. The Father, the Son, the Holy Spirit and a vast number of angels are going with us. We will then feel strengthened as we go with such a large army.

Now the king of Aram was at war with Israel. After conferring with his officers, he said, 'I will set up my camp in such and such a place.'

The man of God sent word to the king of Israel: 'Beware of passing that place, because the Arameans are going down there.' So the king of Israel checked on the place indicated by the man of God. Time and again Elisha warned the king, so that he was on his guard in such places.

This enraged the king of Aram. He summoned his officers and demanded of them, 'Will you not tell me which of us is on the side of the king of Israel?'

'None of us, my lord the king,' said one of his officers, 'but Elisha, the prophet who is in Israel, tells the king of Israel the very words you speak in your bedroom.'

'Go, find out where he is,' the king ordered, 'so I can send men and capture him.' The report came back: 'He is in Dothan.' Then he sent horses and chariots and a strong force there. They went by night and surrounded the city.

When the servant of the man of God got up and went out early the next morning, an army with horses and chariots had surrounded the city. 'Oh, my lord, what shall we do?' the servant asked.

'Don't be afraid,' the prophet answered. 'Those who are with us are more than those who are with them.'

And Elisha prayed, 'O Lord, open his eyes so he may see.' Then the Lord opened the servant's eyes, and he looked and saw the hills full of horses and chariots of fire all around Elisha.

As the enemy came down towards him, Elisha prayed to the LORD, 'Strike these people with blindness.' So he struck them with blindness, as Elisha had asked.

Elisha told them, 'This is not the road and this is not the city. Follow me, and I will lead you to the man you are looking for.' And he led them to Samaria.

After they entered the city, Elisha said, 'LORD, open the eyes of these men so that they can see.' Then the LORD opened their eyes and they looked, and there they were, inside Samaria.

When the king of Israel saw them, he asked Elisha, 'Shall I kill them, my father? Shall I kill them?'

'Do not kill them,' he answered. 'Would you kill men you have captured with your own sword or bow? Set food and water before them so that they may eat and drink and then go back to their master.' So he prepared a great feast for them, and after they had finished eating and drinking, he sent them away, and they returned to their master. So the bands from Aram stopped raiding Israel's territory.

(2 Kings 6:8–23)

Elisha was a man who understood the role of angels, while in contrast his servant was blind and ignorant. With his lack of understanding, the servant was in total fear. Yet amid his fear he knew the only answer was to cry to the man of God for help. 'Lord, open his eyes,' was Elisha's prayerful response. Immediately the servant got a glimpse into the supernatural realm and saw God's mighty warriors, an impressive army of angels. They were so numerous that the words of Elisha must have been ringing in his ears. 'Those who are with us are more than those who are with them' (2 Kings 6:16).

God sent the angels to deliver the man of God, displaying the majestic care He had for Elisha. God changed the situation around, so the enemy army was led away into captivity. Elisha saw God restoring the enemies' sight; he fed and released them with a message for the king of Syria. Those who know their authority can afford to be merciful, kindly. We too have a choice to make: either to be like Elisha and look beyond the circumstances and see into the spiritual realm, or to be like the servant, who was guided by the problems and difficulties. If fear is allowed a foothold then defeat is inevitable, but the truth of God's Word never changes: there are more for us than against us.

We are involved in a great cosmic war. This war rages all around us, day and night. Some are more aware of this battle than others.

When we are born again, we move out of the kingdom of darkness (Satan's kingdom), and into the kingdom of light (God's kingdom). We have a new king but the old king still exists, ruling the world, so warfare is guaranteed. We have to be confident that there are more for us than against us. We may become aware of the power of the devil, and it is easy to get our thinking out of proportion. We can start to see the devil as big and strong; we may even wonder, 'Where is God?' We need to know, like Elisha, that 'Those who are with us are more than those who are with them.'

The Power of Angels

A group of fifty of us held a month's mission in Copenhagen, Denmark. It is a wild place, and when we visited a lawless place called Christiana we knew we could be in danger. Those who lived there were known to burn Bibles and to throw out any Christians who dared to invade their space. I was talking to some drug addicts when they set their dog on me. I was not concerned until I heard my trousers ripping, and I rebuked the dog in the Name of Jesus. A young man, reputed to be the youngest bank robber in Copenhagen, slipped out of the crowd, picked the bull-dog up by the tail and the scruff of the neck, and threw it away from me. When another man threatened us with violence, the same young man again came out of the crowd and punched him. He ran away, bleeding profusely. We were protected by God's angels in that place.

Joyce, my wife, had a similar experience of angels in a time of need.

> On one of our trips to Singapore I took the women of the team to lead a meeting. On our return journey in the car, there was a loud noise and we lurched to the side of the road. It was scary and we jumped out, wondering what had happened.
>
> One of the team shouted, 'Look, the tyre has burst.' Another of the girls asked the driver, 'We need a spanner and a jack. Do you have them?'
>
> The driver replied, 'I don't know, I have borrowed this car.'
>
> We opened the boot, where we had stored our guitars and books, and removed everything looking for the tools, but we could not find anything! It was the middle of the afternoon and the place was deserted. We were on a long straight road and nobody was around for as far as we could see. 'Lord, help us, we have to be on time as we have to meet the men for the meeting,' was our heartfelt cry to God. Suddenly we saw a young man jogging. I remember thinking, 'Where did he come from?' Although it was very hot, he was not sweating. He smiled and said, 'You have a puncture. Do you need some help?'
>
> We all said, 'Yes, but we can't find the things that we need to change the tyre.'
>
> He replied, 'Yes, you can. Look!'

He put his hand inside the car boot, lifted some of the things out of the way and took out a tyre. Then he took out a jack. Quickly he changed the tyre. We were busy returning our belongings to the boot of the car and turned to say thank you, but he wasn't there! It was a straight road and there was no way he could have run out of sight so quickly.

We looked at each other and said, 'Wow! He must have been an angel.' We remembered that there had been a presence of God when he was there; a peace. God had sent an angel to help us in a time of need.

There are so many stories in the Bible about angelic protection. In the Old Testament, the pagan leaders set Daniel up and had him cast into the lions' den. I love that story, it is one of my favourites. The king likes Daniel so much, but he has been trapped into putting Daniel into the lions' den. He can't sleep all night because he knows that anyone who goes into a pit with lions will be overpowered and die instantly. At first light, the king runs to the lions' den to speak to a dead man.

'Daniel, has the God whom you serve been able to deliver you?'

'Oh yes!' says Daniel, 'I am all right. God has shut the lions' mouths!'

The angel had stopped the mouth of the lions. Daniel was pulled out and the other leaders were thrown in: they were killed immediately by the marauding lions.

A Guardian Angel

Angels are able to help us in any situation we face. Pauline Grainger, of Horsham, West Sussex, tells how she panicked when she parked her car and saw smoke pouring from the engine.

Nobody stopped to give me a hand, so I tried to open the bonnet, but could not release the catch. A moment later a petite lady in her early sixties approached me, placed her hand on me and asked, 'Are you in trouble?'

'Yes, I am. I don't know what to do. I am unable to lift the bonnet and there is smoke coming out of the engine,' I replied. By now I was almost in tears.

The lady looked at me and said, 'Don't worry. You don't need to be frightened, I am here to help you.' She lifted up the bonnet. 'Everything is fine,' she said. 'The fire is out, the flames and smoke have stopped.'

The car was fine, there was nothing wrong with it. 'Any time you are in trouble, I will be there to guide and help you,' she told me. I turned to thank her, but she had disappeared.

From the moment we awake until we go to sleep at night, and even while we are asleep, angels watch over us to protect us. They will fight for you, your children and your babies. What love God has for each one of us!

A man was once telling how his little boy of two or three got out of the front gate and disappeared. The man looked for him, but to no avail. There was a motorway on the left and a park on the right. He asked the Lord, 'Which way has he gone?' The Lord answered, 'Go left.' He went left, and there was the little boy, sitting on the bank of the motorway. By now the father was worried: if the child wandered on to the motorway he could easily be killed. When he reached his son, the boy said, 'Daddy, can you see that man there?' He looked everywhere but couldn't see anyone. The boy said, 'There, that man came and tied up my legs.' Children and babies are protected by angels.

God's Elite Force

Angels are highly organized. They differ in size, strength and rank, with a chain of command and a chief angel. Perhaps the lesser angels are learning on the job, like us! Originally there were two archangels but, with the fall of Lucifer, there is now only the archangel Michael. 'Archangel' simply means chief, principal or great angel. Michael is in charge of administration in God's creation, and his special concern is Israel and the people of God who live there.

Gabriel (Hebrew for 'God's hero') is often mentioned in scripture. Gabriel was sent to give messages, and his messages were always concerning Jesus Christ the King. Gabriel came to Mary, the mother of Jesus, to proclaim Jesus' birth. Gabriel will come again to declare the return of Jesus to the earth.

Next come the Seraphim and Cherubim. They are apparently smaller angels, but not like painted, fat babies! As Billy Graham says in his book, *Angels, God's Secret Agents,*

> *The word 'seraphim' may come from the Hebrew root meaning 'love'*
> *(though some think the word means 'burning ones or nobles'). We find*
> *the seraphim only in Isaiah 6: 1–6. It is an awe-inspiring sight as the*
> *worshipping prophet beholds the six-winged seraphim above the*
> *throne of the Lord.*
>
> *The ministry of the seraphim is to praise the name and character*
> *of God in heaven. Their ministry relates directly to God and His*
> *heavenly throne, because they are positioned above the throne. They*
> *are constantly glorifying God. We also learn from Isaiah 6: 7 that God*
> *can use them to cleanse and purify His servants.*
>
> (*Angels, God's Secret Agents*, Billy Graham, London, Hodder & Stoughton, 1976, p.57)

Consider what it must be like to be before the throne day and night in praise and worship. John in Revelation had a glimpse into heaven, and he saw the angels crying out, 'Holy, holy, holy, Lord God Almighty'. While they are worshipping, the seraphim are holding themselves up with the activity of their wings.

As Billy Graham says, 'The Cherubim are always associated with the glory of God. They are found by the throne of God. The Cherubim are the ones guarding the tree of life. After he drove the man out, he placed on the east side of the Garden of Eden cherubim and a flaming sword flashing back and forth to guard the way to the tree of life.' If Adam and Eve had tried to return to the garden a flaming sword would have executed them! Cherubim also guard the mercy seat (Exodus 25: 18). They are guardians of God's glory (ibid., p.59).

Angels' Job Description

Angels always have a clear function and job description. 'Praise the LORD, you his angels' (Psalm 103: 20). This is one of their functions: they praise the Lord, obey every word from God, and do the will of God.

The enemy is too strong for us on our own, but all we have to do is look to Jesus and He will send His angels to deliver us. We need an A team to come alongside and assist us, and the angels will fight with us until the work of God is done. As believers, we can expect the angels to fight for us. 'For he will command his angels concerning you to guard you in all your ways' (Psalm 91:11). This is God's promise: He will do it, not in some ways, but in all our ways.

2 Our Full Salvation

The Angelic Key

Where revival burns, reports of increased angelic activity are pro-lific. For evangelism to succeed the way God intends we must understand how the angels minister and learn to co-operate with them. Jesus replied, 'I will give you the keys of the kingdom of heaven' (Matthew 16:19). We also need to understand what the word 'salvation' means. If you don't understand what you have been saved from and into, how can you present the gospel of Jesus Christ in the full meaning of the word?

'Are they not all ministering spirits sent forth to minister for those who will inherit salvation?' (Hebrews 1:14). We need to lay a foundation so that we can understand the depth of salvation, so we can also understand the role of angels.

The word 'salvation' (*soteria* in Greek) means a full temporal deliverance, to be saved. That word has a full, rich meaning. If salvation was only the forgiveness of past sin that would be fine, but it means much more. It means safety, ease and soundness of mind, that we have been delivered from all evil and the powers of darkness.

When we walk in the glorious fullness of salvation we can then present the fullness of salvation to others. Our sins are for-given, and in the context of salvation our bodies and minds are healed, the wounds are closed. In the ongoing process of being saved we have the eternal life of God within us. When we know our sins are forgiven, we have confidence in the blood of Jesus. 'If we confess our sins, he is faithful and just and will forgive us our sins and purify us from all unrighteousness' (1 John 1:9). When we are convinced of forgiveness, we can present that truth with power to others. This is salvation to its fullest extent.

Salvation includes angels ministering deliverance to the heirs of God. To become an heir of salvation, you need to repent of your sin and acknowledge Jesus died for your salvation. Then you will move from the kingdom of darkness into the kingdom of God.

There is a contrast to what the devil seeks to do. 'The thief comes only to steal and kill and destroy; I have come that they may have life, and have it to the full' (John 10:10). The devil seeks to rob us of this full salvation. Doubt is sent to try to overcome our faith. Many people report that when they became Christians a struggle started. The devil comes immediately to snatch away the Word of God that has been sown into the heart. The demonic powers speak doubt, questioning whether we have really been saved. The things we do or say and the thoughts we have may not be appropriate for a child of God. Many times we have listened to his lies and ended up feeling condemned and wretched, all because we have listened to the voice of doubt. The devil will tempt us to sin, then ask, 'Are you really a Christian?' We sin and also question ourselves about the reality of our salvation.

We need to grow in the truth of God's Word. When we sin we go to God with repentance and ask for His forgiveness. We will no longer allow the devil and his feeble power to make us feel condemned and full of guilt.

Established in Truth

Praise God, we can be established and move on with God. If we sin we have an advocate with the Father: Jesus is our defence counsel. We are not being accused before God; when we repent, He forgives. He cleanses us, we get up and move on with our lives. We don't lie on the ground for three weeks getting our heads kicked in by the devil – instead we get up and move on!

When you have this approach to your salvation, you can impart it to others. 'I am not ashamed of the Gospel because it is the power of God for the salvation of everyone who believes first for the Jew, then for the Gentile' (Romans 1:16). You don't have to have the power in you, you don't have to come up with all the goods. The power of God is in the gospel. For it is the power of the gospel. The power of salvation is released when we share the Word of God with another. The Holy Spirit convicts and convinces on the strength of the Word of God.

Express Your Inheritance

We will want to see people won to Christ. Often we are self-, sin- or Satan-conscious, but God wants us to live life continually Jesus-conscious. We have to get beyond the dictates of self, sin and demons, and look to Jesus, our Saviour. He uses the foolish, despised and rejected, and we don't have to be worthy. It is what Jesus has done and nothing of us that qualifies us for full salvation, and in this we can rejoice. We have a choice to make: the fuller we understand salvation, the easier it will be, and 'with joy you will draw water from the wells of salvation' (Isaiah 12:3). My wife, Joyce, entered into this joy in a new way when she abandoned her embarrassment and self-consciousness to God. She said, 'I don't care, Lord, I want joy anyway and I am going to receive it.' Almost instantly the joy of God's salvation visited Joyce in a fresh new way.

True evangelism is the overflow of the heart. The joy of forgiveness, the peace and assurance of a place in heaven, flows out of a grateful heart. Others will get soaked in the overflow, and many will respond to our God, depending on our availability to God. We have to go beyond our feelings and the things that war against us, because the devil will try and oppose us. We get to the point of acknowledging the life of God flowing through us. We are containers of the glory of God; the treasure of God is within us. We have eternal life, our sins are forgiven, we are co-heirs with Christ. We need to get happy in our salvation and let it show for all to see.

Jesus has given us a new heart and nature: we are no longer of the nature of Adam, but in the nature of God our Father. We have to let our minds catch up with what is happening in the Spirit.

Christ lives in us, Christ in us is the hope of glory. The treasure is inside. Jesus Christ is inside. It is true! Wherever we walk or go, the anointing of God comes upon the people and we can see the miraculous. When Peter walked down the road, they placed sick people under his shadow. Why? Because of the anointing of the Holy Spirit. We need to know God better and the inheritance that is ours in Christ, so we need a Spirit of wisdom and revelation. We are God's children, His servants, His friends, His ambassadors, co-heirs with Christ, and we have inherited all things. 'He who did not spare his own Son, but gave him up for us all – how will he not also, along with him, graciously give us all things?' (Romans 8:32).

Angels on Assignment

When you became a believer, angels were sent to minister to you. How many angels do you have ministering to you personally? As only one-third of the angels fell, two-thirds are still ministering. Angels cannot procreate. The kingdom of God is advancing every day; it is said that seventy thousand people are being born again every day. Now you can see why the devil is so worried. There are more for us than there are against us.

Whenever you dine at a restaurant, a waiter or waitress comes to minister to you, to meet your needs. 'Yes, sir, madam, what can I get you?' This is what God sends the angels to do for us – to wait upon us, the heirs of salvation. They are sent to minister full salvation to us and through us. The angels are sent by God, to wait on us, to minister to us, making sure our needs are met.

If you travel in an aeroplane, it is the safest one in the air because you are in it. You take your angels on it. You can claim that aeroplane for Christ. The place where you are sitting becomes set apart for God. You are not going to crash because you are going to get to your destination. God has a plan, and He has a purpose if you have understanding.

There was a jumbo jet that caught fire and six hundred people died in that fire – everybody except four people. A Christian was in that aeroplane. When the fire broke out, he reported, flesh was dropping off people's bodies. They were melting. He shouted, 'In the Name of Jesus!' and the angels came and moved him along the corridor of the aeroplane. Each time he shouted, 'In the Name of Jesus!' he was moved further along towards deliverance. He saw a hole in the top of the aeroplane. He said again, 'In the Name of Jesus!' and the next thing he knew, he was up, through the hole and on top of the aeroplane. He was able to slide down and escape the flames of the fire. That was salvation in action!

Salvation's Process

Soundness, safety and health are included in salvation (Acts 27: 34; Philippians 1:19). Salvation is described as deliverance from the great flood in Noah's ark (Hebrews 11:7). The spiritual and eternal deliverance is granted immediately by God to those who accept His conditions of repentance and faith in the Lord Jesus (Acts 4: 12). Upon confession of Jesus as Lord, we receive total deliverance from the old sinful nature (Romans 10: 10). There is an assurance of the maintenance of peace and harmony (Philippians 2: 12) and the future deliverance of all His saints in the *paraousia* (the Second Coming).

This salvation is the object of the saints confident of future hope. It means deliverance from the wrath of God, from hell and the lake of fire (Romans 13:11). We (the saints) have already overcome the devil (note the past tense), the devil himself and his demons, by the blood of the Lamb (Revelation 12:11). The holy blood is the agent that procures and keeps us saved through the word of our testimony. Salvation is an ongoing process. We have been saved, we are being saved, and we shall be saved.

Is it any wonder that the writer to the Hebrews says we should see to it that we don't neglect such a great salvation? Is it possible, after all Christ has done, that we can neglect our salvation? Oh yes – casual, uninformed, carnal Christians do so every day. It has been said that two-thirds of the Church does not understand the full meaning of 'salvation'. If this is anywhere near the truth, the Church will need to learn very quickly the full meaning of 'salvation truths'.

Work it out, Saints

'Continue to work out your salvation with fear [reverence] and trembling' (Philippians 2:12). Does that mean we are saved by works? No, no, not like the Jehovah's Witnesses knocking on doors for their place in heaven or the new earth. We are working out what we already have. It is a free gift, with which we do something: we work it out. James tells us, 'Give no place to the devil.' We can choose to give him a place in our lives, because deception will always give a foothold to evil powers. We need a balanced diet of truth and love to walk in the light of Christ's victory.

'Submit yourselves, then, to God. Resist the devil and he will flee from you' (James 4:7). Two key words here: 'submit' and 'resist'. The most important point is to submit. All the resistance in the world will not dispatch the demons; all authority is delegated by God. When we submit to God, delegated authority will flow from Him through us. This releases the power we need to get the job done.

Submission is not a popular subject; many people have differing reasons why they will not submit. It might be because of a warped concept of God, and seeing Him as a tyrannical, abusive authority figure. But anyone who has ever submitted to Father God will know the peace and rest that He brings.

Submit to God

'Your kingdom come, your will be done on earth as it is in heaven' (Matthew 6: 10). Other reasons for a lack of submission to God include pride, rebellion and fear. A preacher once said, 'The one thing that I have learned is that God is smarter than I am.' Pride says: I know best. Many teenagers think they know everything about all subjects and in turn start to instruct their parents. They neither welcome nor accept any advice themselves. Likewise, many Christians behave like this with God: they have a little knowledge about God and His awesomeness, and instead of this producing a humility towards Him, it causes some who are carnally minded to fight and resist God. 'God opposes the proud but gives grace to the humble.' The carnal mind is hostile to God. It says, 'My will is going to override His will.' What a God, that He allows it. Once or twice, I have had weeks of 'run ins' with Almighty God. Eventually I submitted to Him, to be flooded with peace and joy. It left me wondering why I had fought so hard for so long about the surrender of my will.

The need to submit to God is paramount here: it can be the difference between life and death, danger or safety, peace or fear. The fullness of salvation is only truly known when we allow the Saviour to rescue us.

Submission is like two mountain goats walking along a narrow track on a high mountain, trying to pass each other. One of the goats will submit by getting down on his belly, while the other goat will walk right over him. This is the way to pass safely along the ledge to greater adventures. Have you ever submitted your will to God or any human being in this way?

In one sense, we submit every day to rules, regulations and bosses. We can test our reactions. If you are submitted in wisdom (James 3) you will experience life and peace. 'For to be spiritually minded is life and peace' (Romans 8:6, NKJ). You may experience anger and resentment and a bad attitude, and this is a fair indicator that your Godward submission needs working on. If you have a desire for true spirituality, then this is how to get it. Any man or woman who flows in God's genuine authority will have submitted to God at many points. As we submit to God, we can resist the demonic personalities, and something powerful will happen. Resistance is not passive, but aggressive. We use our God-delegated authority, which causes the devil to flee in terror. Make sure you are submitted to God, otherwise the demons will not move at your command.

We Persuade All

Go on the offensive against the demons that bind salvation from sinners. After resistance and enforcement of Christ's victory over them, share your salvation with another person, let it bubble up out of you, overflowing on to those who are blinded. Angels are surrounding and working with you; the fullness of His great salvation is for each of us. We are on our way to heaven, having been delivered from hell's torment, knowing the forgiveness of sins, freedom from the wrath of God. Knowing this, can you really contain yourself and remain silent? We are compelled by His love to persuade all men and bring them into this great salvation.

3 Angels in the Life of Jesus

I was travelling in the front of a car to London with my daughter and two grandchildren. My daughter's boyfriend was driving. My daughter and her boyfriend were having a heated disagreement. As we approached the junction he didn't see the lights were red and drove straight across the junction. I saw a car coming straight for us. There was a tremendous smash as the car hit us on the side and I went unconscious for a matter of seconds. At the moment of impact my daughter and her baby shot head first out of the back window, smashing it as they went through. My grandson was still sitting on the back seat. My legs were trapped under the front dashboard and I was in considerable pain. I could hear my daughter screaming, 'My baby! My baby!'

I tried to get out of the car to help, but I was trapped and the door was jammed. Every movement I made caused a terrible pain to shoot through my body. Suddenly, a man appeared. He ripped off the door with amazing ease, threw it to one side and pulled me out of the car to safety.

The man put us into a taxi and drove us through the middle of London to the nearest hospital. He went into the hospital to tell them what had happened. The staff came out and put me on a trolley and once we had all gone into the hospital he disappeared, leaving no name. I know that was an angel.

Gerry George; Crawley, West Sussex

My Adventure Begins

My adventure in understanding about angels ministering to Jesus came indirectly to me as a young Christian. I was troubled by fear regarding my safety as we travelled into dangerous places around the world. In a study time the Lord began to direct me to the lives of Noah and Jesus. Noah is recorded to have preached righteousness for a hundred years; he was 600 years old when the flood started and 950 when he died. Noah was without a convert (except for his family members). That must have been tough; it is hard to go for a week without making disciples! God began to speak to him about the ark and the flood when he was a mere 500 years old.

Here is the point: 'Now the earth was corrupt in God's sight and was full of violence' (Genesis 6:11). This is not a little corruption or violence – it was filled with violence. Noah preached to these corrupt, violent people, yet no one was allowed to take his life. He was a protected man. 'But Noah found favour in the eyes of the LORD' (Genesis 6:8). This was an amazing revelation that began to change my attitude towards the fear of death. Light began to dawn on me. The devil could not kill Noah in a world filled with violence. Neither could he kill Jesus as a seemingly helpless infant. What about us? Many Christians die prematurely – is this something we must accept and submit to? I don't pretend to know all the answers, but maybe we should take a fresh look.

Gabriel's Message

What a glorious entrance God gave His Son into the earth! Luke records that 'the angel Gabriel was sent by God, to Mary.' She was told: 'You will be with child and give birth to a son, and you are to give him the name Jesus' (Luke 1:31). What a shock for a young girl to see an angel from God! What incredible news! The angel Gabriel had already appeared to Zechariah and announced the birth of John the Baptist who would prepare the way for Jesus (Luke 1:5–20).

The actual birth in a stable may not seem very elaborate, but look at the spiritual activity. Luke records how shepherds were keeping watch over their flocks by night when the angel of the

Lord appeared and stood before them (Luke 2:8–18). The glory of God shone around them and they were greatly afraid. Others who have seen or experienced the glory of God have reported a similar fear. 'Do not be afraid, for behold, I bring you good tidings of great joy,' the angel told them. 'The saviour of the world is born today. Here is where you will find Him.' Suddenly the joyful news is too much for one angel, and a multitude of angels appear, praising God. The shepherds believed the angels, went and found the Messiah and made the news widely known.

The wise men were led to Jesus by a star (Matthew 2:1–12). In Revelation 12 the angels are referred to as the stars of God. Whether it was an angel or a moving star, that is spectacular.

The life of Jesus begins with a death threat, and we have seen how angels are still protecting people from danger. Some of those who are mightily used by God tell of life-threatening experiences in the womb or to them as young babies. 'I will put enmity between you and the woman, and between your seed and her seed. He shall bruise your head, and you shall bruise his heel' (Genesis 3:15). This refers to Mary's seed, Jesus. He was the one to bruise and tread Satan underfoot, at the cross.

An angel of the Lord was protecting Jesus. The angel spoke to his father, Joseph, with direct and clear instructions for his safety. An angel spoke the words of God, Joseph obeyed and Jesus was safe. Draw a parallel to all our lives. We each have a guardian angel. He is willing and ready to give direct and clear instruction for our welfare. We need to believe this. How would we have reacted in Joseph's situation? Would we obey such revelation? If we are willing to obey the voice of God through His angels, we will be saved from the violence on the earth and from the demonic spirits of premature death.

'This is what the LORD says: "A voice is heard in Ramah, mourning and great weeping, Rachel weeping for her children and refusing to be comforted, because her children are no more"'(Jeremiah 31:15). Jeremiah is professing the massacre which took place when Herod ordered the death of all the boys under two. It is an eye-opener to the sceptics. More than three hundred prophecies were fulfilled about the virgin birth, the life, death, resurrection, ascension of the Lord Jesus. I challenge any sceptic to an honest, open study of the Bible for himself. These prophecies were spoken hundreds of years before they happened. There was often great detail and depth in these accounts. One academic, Josh McDowell, decided to disprove the Bible by studying and ridiculing it. He was soundly convinced by the Bible and its many proofs to become a follower of Christ. He has written a book, called *The Evidence that Demands a Verdict* (Alpha, 1990). Take the challenge – do your own study of the Bible, not what others quote or misquote. Reap the reward that many other honest seekers after truth have reaped: eternal life!

When King Herod learned from the wise men of the birth of Jesus he decided to kill the child. The wise men were warned in a supernatural dream not to go back to Herod, and returned to their own country by another way. Now when they had departed, 'an angel of the Lord appeared to Joseph in a dream. "Get up," he said, "take the child and his mother and escape to Egypt. Stay there until I tell you, for Herod is going to search for the child to kill him"' (Matthew 2:13). Herod ordered a mass destruction of all males under two years of age in a futile attempt to kill the baby Messiah.

John reveals in Revelation the struggle that was being fought in the unseen world. He says that the dragon – the devil – stood before the woman about to give birth, ready to devour her child as soon as it was born (Revelation 12:1–17).

'She gave birth to a son, a male child, who will rule all the nations with an iron sceptre. And her child was snatched up to God and to his throne' (Revelation 12:5). Why was Herod so troubled and angry about a mere infant? 'Where is the one who has been born king of the Jews?' (Matthew 2:2). Herod was king of the Jews. Disturbed, he called the Jewish chief priests and scribes. He became even more alarmed to find the Old Testament prophecies were in line with the wise men's account. On this evidence he decided to act. The king had believed the reports of the wise men and the Bible. Their story would seem very wild to some in this day. 'We followed his star,' they said. 'What, you followed a star? Are you nuts?!' There will be more supernatural signs before the second return of Christ. Let us learn to interpret them and the Bible with a degree of wise discernment and faith.

'The woman fled into the desert to a place prepared for her by God, where she might be taken care of for 1,260 days' (Revelation 12:6). This describes the flight to Egypt and gives the exact length of time they stayed there. 'When they [the wise men] had gone, an angel of the Lord appeared to Joseph in a dream. "Get up," he said, "take the child and his mother and escape to Egypt. Stay there until I tell you, for Herod is going to search for the child to kill him"' (Matthew 2:13). The angel not only brought a word of deliverance, he assured them that he would return to tell them when it would be safe to bring Jesus back to Israel. What tender care God took of the baby Jesus.

'When the dragon saw that he had been hurled to the earth, he pursued the woman who had given birth to the male child' (Revelation 12:13). God, through the angels, warned Jesus' parents. God also assisted in their great escape through the angels. After describing the flight to Egypt, John goes on:

> *The woman was given the two wings of a great eagle, so that she might fly to the place prepared for her in the desert, where she would be taken care of for a time, times and half a time, out of the serpent's reach … Then the dragon was enraged at the woman and went off to make war against the rest of her offspring – those who obey God's commandments and hold to the testimony of Jesus.*
>
> (Revelation 12:14, 17)

The wise men's journey was a long one, with many months of preparation and great expense. They arrived with special gifts for the King of the Jews. Mary had believed all the angel told her, and so she was favoured and Jesus was born through her womb.

Delivered from Death

At five years old I became seriously ill with measles. Over a few days I became weaker and weaker, until one night I was looking at the ceiling while at the same time looking at the shape of my body lying under the bedclothes. Suddenly, I was drawn back into my body, aware of blackness and the presence of sin all around.

Into this blackness came a beam of light, and I was drawn towards it. I followed it down a long tunnel until I came to a place of incredible light. It is difficult to describe this light because it was so bright and white. In contrast to the presence of sin was now a place of peace and love. I had never experienced anything like this before. There before me were two figures dressed in white hooded garments. As one of them moved his hood, I saw a face of bronze with red fiery eyes and hair as white as snow. He spoke to me and said, replacing his hood, 'Do not be afraid.'

They started walking towards the source of the light. I knew that this was a place where there was no day or night or sin. The closer we came to the light, the louder the music became. I suddenly realized that

I was leaving my parents behind, so I shouted with everything I could muster, 'NO!' Quickly the angels turned and told me to return to my parents, sweeping me back into my dead body and holding me there. An amazing power came over me – it was like wave upon wave of love. I was transfixed by what was happening. I am so grateful to God for giving me another opportunity to live my life for Him.

Alan Carpenter; Crawley, West Sussex

The Angel of the Lord

At the start of Jesus' public ministry, the Spirit of God led Him into the wilderness to be tempted by the devil. There, after forty days of fasting, the confrontation began. The Holy Spirit brought the 'now' word to Jesus, and with it the spoken word was used to cut and rebuke the devil. After the devil had been defeated, he departed from Jesus for a season. Jesus, being weary with the fast and the heat of battle, needed help. God's angels came and ministered strength to Him. Ministry is one of their many functions. To minister is to serve, to wait at tables, to meet the needs of the one being ministered to. Jesus must have been exhausted, and therefore they would have ministered strength, grace and the ability for Him to fulfil the will of the Father.

After being ministered to by the angels, 'Jesus returned to Galilee in the power of the Spirit' (Luke 4:14). Scripture says that Jesus was full of the Holy Spirit from birth. What was the difference? Before, He was full of wisdom and grace; now, He had returned with power. The results were dynamic.

I have noticed some startling similarities with other men and women of God. The Spirit calls them to a ministry or a breakthrough. Often it begins with a fast, during which confrontation with demonic spirits occurs. When these hindrances are removed, they return 'in the power of the Spirit'. Anyone moving in a powerful anointing would have been confronted before returning in the power of the Spirit. Persevere, saint of God, because the Holy Spirit will bring the 'now' word to your remembrance, enabling you to cut and dismiss the demons with a holy word. The angels will be there to minister to you, making sure you return in one piece in the power of the Spirit with the same dynamic results Jesus experienced.

In the local synagogue He preached from Isaiah 61:1–3. The response was immediate: they were 'filled with wrath and thrust him out of the city, intending to throw him off the cliff edge.' Their intention was murder. I have noticed that the power and the truth of God stirs up men and devils, especially religious devils.

At the onset of His ministry, Jesus faced another death threat. I am so happy life and death are in God's hands, not the devil's. If this was not the case the devil would have killed us moments before we gave our lives to Christ.

The angry mob succeeded in bringing Him to the cliff, but could not push Him over. He walked through the middle of them. No one could touch or manhandle Him. That has to be supernatural – that has to be God! The Bible does not say the angels did it, but someone did! We know the angel of the Lord encamps around those who fear Him, to deliver them. They certainly delivered Jesus. He went His way, to preach the gospel and to do more damage to the kingdom of darkness. What a mighty God we serve!

Later, the Jewish religious leaders sent the temple soldiers to arrest Jesus: hatchet men, hand-picked by the scribes and Pharisees! When they came back without Jesus the leaders were furious. 'Where is He?' they demanded. Sheepishly the soldiers replied, 'Never a man spoke like this man.' He was amazing, every word dripping with the wisdom of God. They were unable to arrest Him, because it was not the time for Him to die. As Jesus Himself said: 'The reason my Father loves me is that I lay down my life – only to take it up again. No one takes it from me, but I lay it down of my own accord. I have authority to lay it down and authority to take it up again' (John 10:17–18).

Angels Minister to Jesus

In the garden of Gethsemane (Luke 22:39–46) a gigantic struggle takes place between the humanity of Jesus and the will of God. The disciples have fallen asleep and He prays alone, facing the cross, a solitary figure in agony. At the height of the struggle, an angel appears and strengthens Him. He needed help; it was not forthcoming from the disciples, but God acted and help came.

The appointed time for His death had arrived. When the guards came to arrest Jesus, Peter cut off the ear of the priest's servant. The fugitive, Jesus, is being arrested, hustled away by the temple guards, but He stops the proceedings to miraculously replace the missing ear. Jesus, looking at Peter, says, 'Put up your sword. If I wanted to, could I not ask the Father to send a legion of angels to deliver Me?' Jesus knew He could ask the Father to release the angels to do what they had done many times before in His life. Now, when death threatened yet again, He did not ask and they did not come, because His time had come.

This was God's glorious master plan – salvation, the rescue of humankind, through the death and resurrection of the Messiah. This is why men were allowed to take, bind, beat and crucify Jesus.

Then came the glorious resurrection. After an earthquake the angel appears (Matthew 28). He not only rolls away the large stone; but is seen sitting on it. That is God's humour. After Jesus has conquered death, hell and Satan, the angel coolly sits outside the tomb on the stone, declaring to all mankind, 'Death, where is your victory?' His countenance was like lightning. And the guards shook for fear of him and became 'as a dead man'. Have you ever watched sheet lightning? It was like that, but constant. I am happy having an angel on my side, but those paid guardians of the tomb were scared out of their wits. If we had been there we would have been tempted to be afraid, as the women were. The angel said to the women, 'Do not be afraid, for I know that you seek Jesus who was crucified. He is not here; for He is risen.'

When Jesus ascended into heaven, angels appeared (Acts 1: 10). They looked like men and were dressed in white clothes, but spoke with authority. 'This same Jesus, who has just ascended into heaven, will return to the same place when the time is right.' He will come back to the Mount of Olives in Israel, there will be an earthquake, and He will go into Jerusalem, to the temple, and destroy the Antichrist with his sword – words – from His mouth. Jesus, the Messiah, will rule the world from Jerusalem. He will set up His kingdom. Hallelujah!

As we have seen, angels played a very integral role in the life of Christ. From the beginning to the end their purpose was to help Him fulfil the will of God. Jesus, the Holy Spirit and the angels succeeded in the execution of God's perfect master plan. They brought great glory to Father God, and now we ourselves are enabled to bring glory to God through their momentous success. God's angels will enable us to fulfil His will, and they will minister and assist us to be presented faultless before the Father on that great day.

I believe God wants us to encounter our angels more than ever before, and we need to believe they are there, ministering to us and for us, seen or not seen. However, the idea that we should dialogue with angels daily doesn't fit into the life of Jesus. He talked daily with His Father. We must tread the wise path and be open to receive the ministry of angels, but with understanding.

Paul, a Witness

But if I live on in the flesh, this will mean fruit from my labour; yet what I shall choose I cannot tell. For I am hard-pressed between the two, having a desire to depart and be with Christ, which is far better. Nevertheless to remain in the flesh is more needful for you. And being confident of this, I know that I shall remain and continue with you all for your progress and joy of faith, that your rejoicing for me may be more abundant in Jesus Christ by coming to you again.

(Philippians 1:22–6, NKJ)

Let's check out some statements about life and death from Paul's own experiences.

Paul was pouring out his heart from prison: 'I want to go home to heaven.' He was yearning with this desire, yet he decided to stay for the sake of his fellow Christians. He made a choice about his own life. He had the power to make this choice, like his Master, Jesus. If we were to trace the life of Paul in the same significant way as that of Christ, we would reach that conclusion, but you will need to dig that out for yourself. Paul's life was a miracle, being spared from death many, many times.

After we had been there a number of days, a prophet named Agabus came down from Judea. Coming over to us, he took Paul's belt, tied his own hands and feet with it and said, 'The Holy Spirit says, "In this way the Jews of Jerusalem will bind the owner of this belt and will hand him over to the Gentiles."'

(Acts 21:10–11)

The prophet Agabus tells Paul about some of the suffering that lies ahead, yet this is not new to Paul. Paul's attitude was amazing. 'Then Paul answered, "Why are you weeping and breaking my heart? I am ready not only to be bound, but also to die in Jerusalem for the name of the Lord Jesus." When he would not be dissuaded, we gave up and said, 'The Lord's will be done' (Acts 21:13–14). They tried to stop him doing God's will, they were well-meaning brethren, but Paul stood his ground. Later Paul was bound in Jerusalem and handed over to the Gentiles, and tradition says he was beheaded in Rome by the Gentiles, as prophesied.

One final scripture regarding Paul: 'Now when there arose a great dissension, the commander, fearing lest Paul might be pulled to pieces by them, commanded the soldiers to go down and take him by force from among them, and bring him into the barracks' (Acts 23:10, NKJ). Paul was about to be pulled apart by an angry mob when the Roman soldiers stepped in and Paul was delivered. But the word of the Lord came: 'Be of good cheer [courage], Paul; for as you have testified for Me in Jerusalem, so you must also bear witness in Rome. And when it was day, some of the Jews banded together and bound themselves under an oath, saying that they would neither eat nor drink till they had killed Paul' (Acts 23:11–12, NKJ). These men took an oath not to eat or drink until they had killed Paul – this was not a light matter but a serious decision on their part. A young man heard the oath and then reported the plot to the commander of the garrison, who made the decision to move Paul and give him protection with 200 soldiers, 70 horsemen and 200 spearmen. This is the God Paul served and we also can serve. Who is in control of Paul's life? Paul's destiny was not to die in Rome at that time, but to testify about the Lord.

God's Heroes Witness

'Some escaped the edge of the sword, out of weakness were made strong, became valiant [brave] in battle, turned to flight the armies of aliens. Women received their dead raised to life again. Others were tortured, not accepting deliverance, that they might obtain a better resurrection' (Hebrews 11:33–5). Their deliverance was available, but they refused it, so it appears that they had a choice.

The golden key is to ask, 'Did they do this by faith?' Those who were delivered chose to be delivered by faith; the same is true of those who chose death in faith for a better resurrection. We have these witnesses, so can we choose to live for ever? No, of course not, but we can choose to live, to fulfil the will of God and bringing blessings to humankind.

Jesus Has the Keys

'I am He who lives, and was dead, and behold, I am alive for ever-more. Amen. And I have the keys of Hades [hell] and of death' (Revelation 1:18). Jesus is our Saviour, He lives again, just as He said. 'I have authority to lay [my life] down and I have authority to take it up again' (John 10:18). He is not only alive for ever-more, but as the second Adam He took on the devil, the strong man (Matthew 12), crushed (bruised) him, trod him under His feet. He took back the keys from Satan, so that Satan does not have the keys to his own home – hell. 'For this reason the gospel was preached even to those who are now dead, so that they might be judged according to men in regard to the body, but live according to God in regard to the spirit' (1 Peter 4:6). No wonder the devil cannot kill us: Jesus has the keys of death, not the devil.

No More Fear

'Since the children have flesh and blood, he too shared in their humanity so that by his death he might destroy him who holds the power of death, that is, the devil and free those who all their lives were held in slavery by their fear of death' (Hebrews 2: 14–15). A lot of people, even Christians, live all their lives in fear of death. Fear will paralyse us, making us ineffective and subject to bondage. It is like having prison doors unlocked without the prisoners being aware that the doors are open, so they remain inside. They remain in bondage even though freedom is there for the taking. Jesus has the key and He has unlocked the door. We can be released, get up by faith, push the door and walk in the truth and freedom. We are no longer in bondage to death. We will fulfil our full life-span, fulfil God's purposes for our life. We will no longer be living as paralysed, timid Christians with fear of death because we know with confidence that Christ has set us free.

My wife and I were on honeymoon in Blackpool. We were so much in love that we walked across the road without checking to see if anything was coming. We had reached the halfway point when we saw a van coming towards us. It must have been doing 80 miles per hour, and I thought, 'Lord, this van is going to hit us. Even if he puts his brakes on, he will still hit us!' Suddenly he stopped dead! He didn't put his brakes on, he just stopped. An angel stood before us with his hand out. Praise God, I give Him all the glory and the praise for what He had just done in our lives. Praise Jesus!

John Marshall; south Derbyshire

What God has done for His Son, for the apostle Paul, for the heroes of faith in Hebrews 11, He will do for us. As the psalmist says, He will give us a long life and satisfy us with His salvation (Psalm 91:16).

4 Angels and the Church

In February 1998 Colin Urquhart was at a revival conference along with John Avanzini and Sam Hinn at Enevald Flaten's church in Bergen, Norway, when he had an encounter of the Angel of the Lord's Presence.

The Lord had spoken to me before about the Angel of His Presence. He said, 'Surely they are my people, sons who will not be false to me; and so he became their Saviour. In all their distress he too was distressed, and the angel of his presence saved them' (Isaiah 63:8–9).

The Angel of His Presence is another way of describing the Presence of the Lord, the Lord Himself in scripture. The Angel of the Lord's Presence is the Lord turning up in a particular way, bringing His presence into what is happening.

During a time of praise and worship at a conference in Norway (on an evening I was not preaching), I became aware of the Presence of the Lord. I was expecting to meet with the Lord, but was not expecting the Lord to do what He did. While the worship was going on, I was on my face before the Lord. I was the only one on my face while everybody else was clapping and singing, as that was the kind of worship that evening. God was doing something different with me at that time.

While I was on my face I suddenly saw the Angel of His Presence. I had never, ever seen an angel in this way before, although I have seen angels in human form. The following scripture came to my mind.

'Do not forget to entertain strangers, for by so doing some people have entertained angels without knowing it' (Hebrews 13:2). This has happened previously to me many times. I have seen angelic appearances in human form but never one of these great, glorious angels before that moment. Nobody else saw this, but right there before me was an enormous towering figure and I have to admit being disappointed that the angel had wings. I was disappointed: I really didn't believe the stereotype of angels having wings. To me an angel is a messenger from God, and he doesn't need wings to be a messenger from God! I was humbled by seeing the Angel of the Lord's Presence had wings. This angel was large, so tall, so enormous it is impossible to say how tall. Then His wings enfolded me. God spoke, 'You are under the protection of My wings' – you will know when you are having a genuine meeting with God as scripture will always come to mind. He then lifted me up. This took some time to lift me up, as He was so tall. It was like going up a lift of a skyscraper but there was no lift, only the everlasting arms. I was going up, higher; and higher; and higher; and higher. I knew I was being gripped in the Lord's Presence. I also knew God was not giving me just a nice experience. Every time I have met with God, every time I have seen the Lord, there has always been a consequence and this was not going to be an exception. The timing is always perfect in God's economy (I had once seen the Lord enthroned in glory. I was right before the throne of God, and saw the Lord as Isaiah did). I realized that seeing the Angel of the Lord's Presence was going to be significant. When the Angel let me go after about half an hour, I sat down. The Lord said to me, 'Look at that scripture again.' I opened my Bible and looked at the verse.

'And the angel of his presence saved them. In his love and mercy he redeemed them; he lifted them up and carried them all the days of old' (Isaiah 63:9). Well! If I hadn't been sitting down I would have fallen down! Although I had read the verse about the Angel of the Lord's

Presence, it didn't connect while that vision was going on, about being lifted and carried. God did it, not imagination on my part. It happened and then I saw it in scripture. This was what I have been waiting for. It was obviously God's timing for a particular reason.

The following day whilst I was praying in my room, the Angel of the Lord's Presence turned up again. The previous evening after the above meeting, the Angel of the Lord's Presence was with me again as I was going to sleep. I awoke the following morning with the Angel of the Lord's Presence with me. I knew something was going to happen. I had never seen the Angel of the Lord's Presence before but now I saw Him three times. While praying in my room, the Lord took me to the following scripture, Luke 12, and after reading this passage, I was totally gripped in the Lord's Presence for three hours. I could hardly move! During these three hours the Lord kept impressing upon me what to preach that evening. God was unfolding it, and He kept going over it again and again. I am used to the Lord giving me messages, normally it is while I am preaching; but not like this, beforehand. I have never known a time of preparation like this before a meeting. The Lord told me to focus the meeting on the kingdom. The kingdom of God in scripture is both present and future.

As I was preaching I used an illustration of two chairs. One chair represented the believer and the other chair the unbeliever. The Lord told me to sit on the unbeliever's chair and DIE!! The Lord showed me how to do it and I did it. I stood in the middle of the platform and collapsed! Afterwards I woke up, coming before the Lord in heaven, I bowed the knee and said, 'Jesus, you are Lord, Jesus, you are Lord.' Then immediately and with a great shock, I was thrust back on the chair. The Lord told me what to say. 'What do you mean, Lord?' 'Not everyone who says to me, "Lord, Lord," will enter the kingdom of heaven, but only he who does the will of my Father who is in heaven. Many will say to me on that day, '"Lord, Lord, did we not prophesy *in your name, and in your name drive out demons and perform many miracles?" (Matthew 7:21–2). What do you mean that you don't know me? 'They also will answer, "Lord, when did we see you hungry or thirsty or a stranger or needing clothes or sick or in prison, and did not help you?"'(Matthew 25:44).*

God was in that meeting! Then I was slumped on the chair. When I woke up, I said, 'O Lord, thank God it was only a dream.' I threw myself on the chair. I had a white sweater on the chair to signify the Lord's pure robe. I grabbed hold of the sweater and hugged it and said, 'O God, I am so sorry, I am so sorry that I wasn't ready. I am so sorry that I gave up. I am so sorry that I didn't obey Your Word. I am so sorry that I went to all the meetings and heard the Word, went forward and got prayed for but didn't realize that there was anything You wanted me to do. I am so sorry, Lord.' There was an electric atmosphere in the place. It was the atmosphere of the Angel of the Lord's Presence there. The Presence of the Lord is not just nice, He is awesome. I then said to the people, 'Of course, the only trouble is that when Jesus said these things He wasn't talking about a dream. Let us pray.' Many were in tears, some fell on their faces as God broke though and touched everybody's heart.

Angels' Church Attendance

In the book of Revelation, John tells how he was told to write to the angels of the churches of Ephesus, Smyrna, Pergamum, Thyatira, Sardis, Philadelphia and Laodicea. These churches each had an assigned angel.

The Church is not a building, but it is the 'called-out ones', those who through repentance and faith have joined themselves to Christ; and the true church is a place of constant protection. Jesus is the head of this Church: we are His body. It is a living, pulsating, vital organization filled with God's eternal life. When we join the Church we become protected people.

Revival Reports

Revival is now reported in Argentina, but before it started the Holy Spirit invaded a Bible college and disrupted it. The students started praying, and this went on for the next three or four months with repentance, conviction of sin and awareness of God's holiness. The students wept, with pools of tears appearing on the floor around them, and prayed for Argentina, which in those days was known as the graveyard for ministers. The promises were hard to believe, but look what God has done – revival has come to Argentina.

One of the young men from the Bible School was walking and praying in the woods when he met an angel. This angel was so big, majestic and powerful he was scared and ran away, but the angel ran after him! That young man ran into a house and shut the door, but the angel walked through the door. He had a reason for running; he was running away from God. If you meet angels, in the holiness of God, you become aware of your own shortcomings. If you have an encounter with God you realize how unholy you are. The angel confronted him, talked to him, and the student repented and got right with God. Involvement with angels is serious stuff.

Each of the churches in Revelation is commended for certain things, and told how they must take action on other things. One church was told they had lost their first love, and had to repent, turn around and come back to their first love or else their 'candlestick' would be removed. Many churches fight with each other, because they have a lack of understanding. Unless there is unity and a love of the churches, the angel will be bound to limited action, or could even be removed. Sadly, there are churches where the presence of God has departed: the candlestick has been removed, and the angel of the Lord is not there any more. Angels will not stay around to waste their time. They have business to do.

Angels: Use Them or Lose Them

If we are not doing something with our angels, they will move to another church that is doing God's will. You have to make the decision to be obedient to God, then the angels will be involved with you. The seven churches of Revelation, where the angel and the glory left, are ruins today. It could have been so different if they had responded to God's rebukes. Let us learn from their mistakes. Let us fear God, lest the angel of His presence and the glory be removed from us!

Unity is important, and if we have anything in our heart that needs to be sorted out, let us sort it out. If there is anything in our hearts that is bitter or resentful, disrespectful to the people in authority, we must ask the Lord to forgive us now and get it out of the way. Do business with God. If we are in disunity we open the Church to enemy activity.

One of the hallmarks of holiness is thanksgiving. If we are a thankful people we are in a good place. This is one of the fruits of holiness. Start, by thanking God for the angels you have in your church.

Jesus, Our Apostle and High Priest

'Let us not give up meeting together as some are in the habit of doing' (Hebrews 10:25). It is important to understand the role of the Church. Do not neglect to meet together as the Church. What bodily parts go off, leaving the rest of the body impaired? It is imperative to recognize together the role of the Church, to unite ourselves to its function and expression. It will save our lives.

If there is not a protective hedge around the Church, why did Paul put out of the Church the one who was in immorality, over to Satan? Even when he was committing immorality, in the Church he was still under the umbrella of God's protection. When finally, as a last resort, he was put out of the Church, he was in Satan's territory. He was no longer afforded the protection of the Church. All of the grace, anointing, five-fold ministry covering, everything that Jesus had put there, was withdrawn from this unrepentant man. He ran into trouble. Satan was now able to attack and assault him at will. Only then did the man get scared: he quickly repented, left his sin and returned to the Church for protection. Why do you think the devil seeks to get us out of the Church? I am not talking about going to a dead church or going to a church just because of loyalty. Find a church with a bit of life in it. Once we get established in a church, we live under God's protection.

God is so merciful, kind and good to all. It is not something God forces on us. God knows what works, folks. God knows what is best for us. When He tells us to go to church, we should run to church! That is the place of refuge. I have learned more in the last four years, since joining Kingdom Faith Ministries. I am aware of an apostolic grace and anointing. We need to look for the apostolic covering in these days.

The churches in Ephesus, Smyrna, Pergamum, Thyatira, Sardis, Philadelphia and Laodicea had an angel looking after them. If you multiply this with the angels who look after believers, those who look after the babies, in this dangerous world the Church is the best place to be!

God Expects Respect

It was after Christmas, January 1998. I was standing on a chair in my bedroom taking down the last of my Christmas decorations. The chair I was standing on was a wooden one with a high, broad back and a smooth polished surface. I was wearing a pair of old socks to keep my feet warm. Lazily and foolishly I didn't bother to remove them before climbing on to the chair.

As I was standing on tip-toe trying to remove a stubborn drawing pin, my foot slipped and skidded from under me. I was flung forward, causing my body to lurch backwards. As I fell, my weight continued to carry me backwards and the thought flashed through my mind that this could be a serious fall and I might injure my spine. I felt my back hit the tip of the chair-back and my legs flailed high in the air, level with the chair-back. As I fell, I knew I had passed the point of regaining my balance, and if my back didn't take the full brunt of the fall, I would end up flipping backward, head first, landing on the hard wooden floor. I also thought how the corner of my small wooden chest of drawers was protruding somewhere below me, and how I could easily catch my head on it as I fell.

As I had these thoughts, it was as if invisible hands caught me, and suddenly I was set upright on the chair. I stood there amazed and stunned. The scripture came to mind: 'He will command his angels concerning you to guard you in all your ways; they will lift you up in their hands, so that you will not strike your foot against a stone' (Psalm 91:11–12). In that instant I knew that the Lord had sent His angels and they had caught and lifted me in their heavenly arms and set me down safely. I had a strong sense of them hovering around me.

There are times when we need wisdom in the things we do. I should have removed my socks before climbing on to the chair. Yet the Lord still watches over us when we are being careless or lazy. I take great comfort in knowing His angels are with me in my home, and whatever I am doing there they are sitting, flying around the house, watching me.

Corrina Yeo; Horsham, West Sussex

The angel is representing something in the church set-up that is going to be protective. Angels will speak into our lives, as well as the Holy Spirit, to get us into the will of God. Angels are not the kind of beings that we want to make jokes about. I am not saying that they are morbid – Jesus was fun. The father will play with his children on the floor, but when it comes time to go to bed the father uses his authority. With Jesus there is both fun and authority. With the holy angels we have to be in awe, too. Respect the Church of Jesus Christ, honour and love her.

Prophet Bill Hammond described a situation with a pastor. This pastor was being abused by a lady in his congregation. She would openly challenge him, speak badly of him and even attack him physically and verbally. She did this for a full three years. It got to the point where he said, 'Lord, I just cannot take any more.'

Aren't you glad you don't have all the problem people in your church? You will have a number, but God is so gracious He has shared them around!

The visiting prophet called this lady forward. He told her what she had been doing and that she needed to repent and get right with the pastor. She fell on her face and cried out to God for mercy. The other people had their heads under the chairs, repenting and saying, 'Lord, don't call me out!' Hallelujah.

Angels are to be respected. They are not equal with God in power and strength. They are created beings. They are given power by God.

To each local church, God has assigned a powerful angel to look after that church. We are surrounded by God's élite team of minders. The ministry of angels is to protect us so that we can fulfil the will of God. Understand the involvement of angels in your church, revere the things of God, and it will be well with you.

The True Church

After I studied, thought and prayed about it, my conclusion was that some Christians have no concept of true Church. The true concept is that the Church is supernatural: it is living in a spiritual dimension as well as a natural dimension. People have a preference for flitting from one church to another. They have the attitude, 'If I want to, I will stay here. If I am upset, then I will vote with my feet. I am gone.' Who is Lord? The people or God? Sadly, often it is the people, and many churches are weak and anaemic because of this.

Leaders are imperfect. We may see things that are wrong. Do not let that stop us. When we let God choose the church for us, we can stay put and carry on being faithful and loyal. God will exalt and promote us in due season, as long as we don't fall out and start fussing with people. God will exalt us as we do things in secret, for He sees what we do. We are talking about a supernatural realm where the Church governs and the people are under the Lordship of Christ. God made the true Church. Let us love the Church and respect the people in it! We need to love what Jesus loves and hate what Jesus hates. Jesus loves the Church. If we do not love the Church we have a problem with Him. I am talking about the true Church. We are to love the Church. We do not have to judge the Church – Jesus is the judge. We are not judge, jury and executioner. We do not want that job. Do not be the one who walks around being the prophet to the churches – unless God has truly called you to do it.

Salvation's Power

'Therefore He is also able to save to the uttermost those who come to God through Him, since He always lives to make intercession for them' (Hebrews 7:25, NKJ). Do you realize He is saving each of us to the uttermost today? When I got a revelation of that, I went bananas. Whoopee! In other words, He is saving me. He is holding me. He is keeping me even from all those things that are confronting me and tempting me, and from whatever else comes against me. That means to the utter, utter, uttermost. Have you ever been to the uttermost? I don't suggest that you go there, but sometimes we are heading in that direction and Jesus is still saving us. He is still our Saviour. He is ever-living to make intercession for us. He is saving us in the valley. He is saving us on the mountain top.

Our angels are responding to the saving power of Jesus, to His intercessions, to keep us from falling and present us to the Father blameless. We have angels with us. If we could have our spiritual eyes opened, we would see them and they would be there right beside us. Some of us would not be alive if our angels were not protecting us.

'Therefore, holy brothers, who share in the heavenly calling, fix your thoughts on Jesus, the apostle and high priest whom we confess' (Hebrews 3:1). He calls us holy; it would be wonderful if the whole Church really believed this was true.

One of the ways to release angels is to recognize who Jesus is. One of Jesus' high-priestly ministries is making intercession in heaven for us, and the angels operate through the intercessions of Jesus Christ. Jesus is working in heaven right now as our High Priest. When we pray, the angels go into operation. How much more when Jesus begins to pray!

We have a personal angel who knows our name. From birth, Jesus had a personal angel: the angel of the Lord. We have a personal angel who is commissioned to look after us. We will be assigned other angels, especially when we get involved with the will of God, and we will need more angels to come with flaming swords to do strong warfare; angels will certainly come and fight on our behalf. But what we are doing must be in agreement with what Jesus is praying, otherwise we will bind our angels and hinder them from working: they work in answer to the intercessory prayers of Jesus Christ.

Intercessions with Jesus

When we pray, the angels go into operation, so how much more when Jesus begins to pray! Every day consider and then confess Jesus as your High Priest. Do you know what He is doing for you in heaven right now as your High Priest? Our names are engraved on the palms of His hands. He is presenting us before the Father every day as our High Priest – our names, being presented before God, by Jesus. God was boasting about Job: 'Have you seen My servant Job? There is nobody righteous like him.' Jesus is boasting about us in heaven. He is presenting our names before the Father in heaven.

This is wonderful; this is the ministry of the High Priest. The High Priest offers a sacrifice: Jesus has offered the sacrifice of Himself, His own life, once and for all, so that we can go and meet Him in the holy place. Wonderful, isn't it? He is ever-living to make intercession for us. Have you confessed Jesus as your Saviour, your Healer, your Apostle? Did you ever confess Him as your High Priest? There is much more that He is doing in heaven.

His high-priestly role includes advocacy on our behalf. He is our advocate, our defence counsel. Have you ever been accused? Jesus is our advocate. On one of our missions, a lawyer on the team started to accuse me of certain things. I wanted to go and fight with that person and sort it out. Have you ever asked for five minutes off from God?

A man rushed towards a preacher in an auditorium. This man punched the preacher. The preacher punched him back, knocking him out with one punch. He said, 'I took a few minutes off and repented afterwards!' Dear Lord! I felt like doing the same with this person. God said to me, 'I am your advocate and your defence counsel. I am your legal representation.'

I said, 'Well, you don't seem to be doing much about it.' You don't talk to God like that, do you?

He said to me, 'I am going to do something about it, but I want you to stop doing something about it first.'

Sometimes that is what God waits for, isn't it? I stopped fussing and arguing. I was still in pain, but was getting to a place where I was believing Jesus to be my advocate. He told me, 'After three days I will start operating.'

After three days it was amazing. He started being my advocate. I didn't do or say anything. The whole thing changed and turned back on that person. The truth prevailed; I was totally vindicated. This is another of His high-priestly roles: He is our advocate.

If you come from the same background as me, you had to learn to fight to survive. Any of you ever had to fight to survive? When we become Christians, it is a shock to be told, 'Don't fight for your rights any more. Let God fight for you.' Well, I mean, He is actually much bigger than us, anyway. He is our Daddy, isn't He? If you pick on me, you are picking on my dad, you are picking on my family. He is able to sort things out.

I am referring to fighting for our rights with anger and resentment in a soulish, carnal way. This is to be avoided at all costs. There is a fight of faith, a warfare in the spirit that is often accompanied by action. The fight to abolish slavery was spearheaded by God-fearing reformers. Martin Luther King led the civil rights struggles. These God-fearing men and women did not carry this fight in the soulish realm, but as a just crusade for God, that God honoured and blessed. In an age that demands its rights on every issue, let us discern the difference between selfish ambition and godly crusades. It is true to say that if you fight for your rights and God's not fighting for you, you are by yourself. Rest your case and let God arise and fight for you.

I have received Jesus as my Saviour, as my Healer, as my Righteousness, and now I have received Him as my High Priest and Apostle. Have you received Jesus as your High Priest and Apostle? That brings an anointing. Was there ever a prayer of Jesus that was not answered? The prayer Jesus prayed about unity will be answered. Aren't you glad! Why don't you start prophesying unity instead of begging? God, give us unity. Stand up and declare to the devil of disunity: 'Get out, in Jesus' Name!' Put the angels to work against disunity. Instead of being part of the problem, be part of the solution.

I once went to my pastor and I told him about a situation that was happening between another guy and myself. We were fussing with each other. He said to me, 'Dave, are you part of the problem or are you part of the solution?' Do not be part of the problem: be the answer. If your church is not what you want it to be, then go and change it!

You can stand in front of your church and declare: 'In the Name of Jesus, spirit of disunity, get out of this church. The angels are moving in. Jesus Christ is Lord over this church.' You are part of the solution, not part of the problem, because Jesus is praying for that church. Listen to what Jesus is praying for that church and join Him – be in agreement. You are agreeing and confessing that He is your High Priest. You are united with His prayers. You are releasing the angels to do the will of God, releasing the angels to answer the prayers of Jesus for unity.

Agreement with Jesus

What do you think Jesus is praying for our families right now? What do you think He is praying for our church right now? It is not what we may think. When the Samaritans would not receive Jesus the disciples said, 'Lord, shall we call down fire?' The fire did come, but it was not the fire that the disciples were asking for. The fire came later, in the encounter with the woman at the well, and when it came it was the fire of God. What are the intercessions of Jesus?

As a young believer, I saw the news on television that a bomb had killed 19 people in a UK city. The news caused me to rise up in anger and indignation. It was an outrage, a horrific event. I was a young Christian, rising up in anger and judgement, like everybody else in the room. All of a sudden I began to cry. Out of my heart I began to pray for the Irish people in this country. I began to intercede and pray along a certain line for the protection of the Irish people. The next day, some people took bombs and threw them into the Irish pubs. Incensed English people went and attacked innocent people with bombs and fists. People were getting beaten up – even Irish butter was banned. God had me interceding, praying for those innocent people. These were in part, at least, the intercessions of Jesus. It was not what I heard on the news, not what was in my mind.

How often our mind can be going in one direction and God's spirit in another direction. Gerald Coates was prophesying over some Salvation Army officers, saying, 'Revival is coming to you,' and telling them the way it was going to happen. He told them all this from the Holy Spirit. Yet his mind was going in another direction: he was thinking, 'I should be telling them to get out of that dead set-up and get into a live church.' His mind was going in one direction, but he was prophesying out of his spirit. He was surprised at the words coming out of his mouth. God has been moving powerfully in the Salvation Army. God said to him, 'I am not interested in your opinions, Gerald!' We would do well to take note: God is not interested in our opinions.

Praying with Jesus

Jesus is praying, but not always for the things we think we want. We can be praying for our spouse to change, but we might not be praying the intercessory prayers of Jesus. Jesus might be praying for you to change!

Many years ago, my wife's father was hospitalized; the doctors said he was dying. Joyce had become a Christian at 12 years of age, and she was always praying to God for her dad to be changed. Her father often beat his wife; an alcoholic, he drank and wasted all the money. Joyce was praying, 'Lord, change him, save him.'

One day God revealed to Joyce the need to forgive her father. The intercession of Jesus changed her heart. This was a big struggle for Joyce, because of the tremendous bitterness in her heart since childhood. Joyce wrote a letter to her father, asking for his pardon and forgiveness of her bitter attitude towards him, with the grace and help of God.

At that very time, an Indian evangelist visiting West Malaysia received a word of knowledge from God to visit the local hospital. The man did not know Joyce or her family. On his arrival at the hospital the Lord instructed him to turn right, to turn left, 'and that is the man there you are to pray for!' It was Joyce's father. The evangelist walked into his room and cast the demons out of him. This evangelist is a very bold man. Joyce's father was instantly healed and came to know Jesus as his personal Saviour.

Her father wrote to Joyce, asking for her forgiveness. Joyce's father had not previously written to her; they had had no real communication since her arrival in England many years before. Joyce's letter was going over in the post to West Malaysia and his letter came over at the same time – the letters crossed in the post! Hallelujah. His letter told about his salvation and healing. The impact on his life was so great, he asked Joyce for forgiveness of all the past abuses.

Joyce learned that we can bind people by not forgiving them. Even though we may be praying for them to change, nothing changes. Joyce learned she could loose her father to God. Once it was in God's hand, He was able to release His servant and His angels. The outcome was glorious. Joyce had responded with agreement to the intercessory prayer of Jesus. Joyce had received a changed heart and character. Her father was raised from his deathbed and gloriously saved. What a God He is! Joyce had agreed with the intercessory prayer of Jesus. Jesus had been praying along that line for a long time before Joyce forgave her dad. He had been bound for a long time.

Isn't it important to move in kingdom dynamics? God knows that forgiveness works. God knows the intercessory prayer that will work. All we have to do is agree with it. Confess that it is true. Agree and let the angels move into the hard situations. Miracles and deliverance will be a normal part of your kingdom lifestyle.

Jesus will inspire us by the Holy Spirit to pray along the lines He prays when we are praying for our church, family or workplace. Meet with God, heart to heart, and we could be praying a different prayer to what we are praying right now. The results will be phenomenal.

The angels are able to stop the mouths of lions. The angels are able to help you in work situations. Daniel was duly promoted and made the prime minister of the nation.

Shadrach, Meshach and Abednego were thrown into a fiery furnace. This story is very special and precious to me. If you have ever been in the fire, you will understand why. They had refused to bow down and compromise by worshipping the image of the king. Jealous leaders went and told the king. The king was hopping mad and put them into a fiery furnace. The furnace was so hot the soldiers who put them in were charred alive. The crowd noticed a fourth person walking around in the flames. The king was astonished, alarmed. 'Any God who can save men in a red-hot fiery furnace has got to be more powerful than any other god,' he exclaimed. Not even the smell of smoke lingered on the exiles.

After the deliverance, they were promoted – that is God's favour. I went through the fire once because I refused to compromise. Some people said to me, 'You are going through the fire because of your pride. You need to repent.' These people even quoted this Bible story to prove their advice was from God. They brought the story about Shadrach, Meshach and Abednego, and said, 'That is what God gave us for you.' That was what God had revealed to me, as well. But they were telling me in a totally different way. The interpretation was flawed: they said the exiles were put in the fire because they were not living right. In fact, they were put in there because they *were* living right. Don't think every time you get into trouble you are not living right. If you live right you will often get into trouble. 'In fact, everyone who wants to live a godly life in Christ Jesus will be persecuted' (2 Timothy 3:12).

There are some things that get us put into the fire. This is not a godly fire – the fire that came against me and attacked me was not a godly fire. The angel of the Lord came in that situation delivered them out from the fire.

If we are in a fire we need to be delivered by the angel of the Lord. The angel of the Lord will come and deliver us out from that fire. When I was in that fire the angel came. I knew when he came and I knew what he did. He delivered me, and after I came out of the fire I was promoted. God promoted me. He will promote you, too! 'When you walk through the fire, you will not be burned; the flames will not set you ablaze' (Isaiah 43:2). When we go through the fire, it seems we will get burned. Imagine walking around in a fire! Sometimes, when we are standing on the Word of God, it is like that, isn't it? We are going down for the third time, then God says, 'Enough is enough,' and He sends an angel to deliver. He said we will not be burned. We will not be drowned. The Word of the Lord will be fulfilled. If you have lived it, you will know what I am talking about. If you haven't been in the fire, let this encourage you when you are.

The only thing that was burned in the fire was their bonds. The things that bound their hands were destroyed. They were not there because of pride, but because of a refusal to compromise.

Involved with Angels

The angels were involved in the Bible in every ministry, with every person. Many stories are recorded for our learning and benefit. Angelic involvement is going to increase, in these end times before the return of Christ. The Holy Spirit will bring a fresh revelation of angels. A fresh revelation of angels to the Church. Some of us are going to see angels as clearly as the noonday sun. Many of us are going to be delivered by angels. My wife and I were transported by angels – we were in one place and then we were in another place that we needed to get to. No travel: we were just there. God uses His

is going to be a revival in the Church and
y, many people are going to come to Christ.
They are going to come in their thousands and eventually in their millions. There are going to be breakthroughs in the television world-wide. The media will be a tool in the hand of God to reach the masses. There will be signs and wonders. A new generation will arise, the Joshua generation with a Joshua anointing, a warrior anointing, a bold anointing. Everywhere this new breed goes, heaven will be released on to the earth. Miracles will be the norm – the Church and the Christians will be restored to normality.

We are at present so far from it. In one of our camps the Spirit of God was moving in a powerful way. The consensus of the people was that God was great and that the camp was marvellous. Now, God has more on His agenda than a powerful camp. God has revival on the top of His agenda. Normal Christianity, according to the Bible, is with the angels: seeing angels, experiencing angelic activity, angels delivering us from evil on every turn. That is normal Christian living. It is not normal to be sceptical, to be those who rationalize and discount the miraculous. That is not normal. It is abnormal. Don't be bound by this kind of thinking any longer. Those who think like this have often debated for years and did not find the truth. Don't be bound by that sort of religious thinking. Be influenced by the Word of God.

A well-known singer was converted to Christ. This famous man was accused of being brainwashed. 'Yes, I am,' he said, 'but at least I am choosing who is washing my brain.' Our brains are being washed. Clean, cleansed, renewed. There is a new thing that God is doing on the earth. We are going to know who we are in Christ. The Church will arise in unity, with purity and purpose. The harvest shall be gathered in and then our Messiah will return.

Angels Know Our Names

'The angel said' (Luke 1:13). He spoke. Many have heard an angel speak and many have heard God speak in an audible voice. The angel spoke audibly to Zechariah: 'Do not be afraid, for your prayer has been heard.' The angel knew Zechariah's name, and he knows our name, too. Have you ever been in a meeting and met someone seven times and still can't remember their name? God know us all; He knows our name.

I was once asked to visit a man dying in hospital. He had been brought here to England with terminal liver cancer and a number of other incurable diseases. His Christian wife had phoned me from Malaysia and asked me to go and pray for him 'He is a Christian, but he needs to be healed,' she had told me. It turned out that he was not a Christian at all. This man started fighting with me because I was talking about the Lord.

After the visit I prayed for him throughout the night, and then in a vision I saw him being born again. The next day he was born again, but he still had a tremendous fear of dying. That night an angel visited him and spoke to him. It is an amazing story, really. The angel spoke to him and called him by his small Chinese name. In England, only his wife knew that small Chinese name. It is a nick-name. Nobody else knew it. The angel spoke audibly in a man's voice. He said, 'Don't be afraid. Everything is going to be all right,' and called him by his small Chinese name. Did you know that God can speak Chinese? That came as a revelation to me! This man was never afraid again after this visitation, and died with great dignity a short while later.

God knows our name. He knows our situation, He knows where we are, He knows how to get us delivered. I want to encourage you: begin to agree with the prayers of Jesus and release your angels to get to work. The angel said to Zechariah, 'Don't be afraid.' That means he was afraid. They had waited a long time for a child. The woman being barren, they had suffered ridicule and misunderstanding. Now the angel said, 'Your prayers have been heard by God in heaven. I am here to deliver the answer: you will have a child. His name will be called John.'

You may remember the angel took twenty-one days to come to Daniel. The angel said, 'On the first day that you prayed, God heard your prayer.' Isn't it incredible – many times we give up and lose heart because there is a time delay. The angel said, 'Don't be afraid. Your prayer is answered; you are going to see the prophet John being born to Elizabeth.' Zechariah did not believe God's words and he was struck dumb for a season. Contrast his response with Mary's. When God's messenger came to Mary, she also asked some questions of the angel. Mary did not have an unbelieving heart: 'Let it be to me according to your Word.' What if an angel came and spoke to you the way he did to Mary: 'You are going to bear a child as a virgin'? That goes against the natural. (You are not going to get that message because there is only one Saviour!) The message was hard to believe, but Mary's response was staggering: she met the word of the Lord with faith. 'Let it be unto your handmaiden according to the word of the Lord.' What would your response be, Zechariah's or Mary's?

The angels fed the prophet, released Peter from prison, strengthened Jesus. They will pour out God's deserved judgement on to the earth. They will separate all mankind at the end of the age. What a great job they do! Angels have not diminished in their ministry. We need to experience much more of them.

I believe that God is going to save whole households in these days, that He is going to send angels to put these connections in place. Are you ready for yours?

A Secure Prison

Peter was delivered by the angel. Peter was in prison, in stocks and chains. James had been killed. It was now Peter's turn: Herod was going to kill him, too. The Church started to pray. Remember, prayer always releases angels into the fray. Angels are released to do the will of God when somebody is praying. As the Church prayed, the angels went into action. Peter's chains supernaturally fell right off. The angel brought Peter to a guarded door. The guards were standing beside the door. The door supernaturally flew open, even though it was locked. Peter just walked right through.

Up to this time the angel had helped Peter. Where he could not help himself, the angel did it for him, but now that Peter was able to do the rest himself, the angel split and left him. Peter walked out, totally free, and knocked on the door of Mary's house, where Rhoda the servant girl answered the door. Rhoda thought it was Peter's ghost. She started screaming and ran away. The angel of the Lord had answered prayer and delivered Peter.

In life-threatening situations, when we pray the angel of the Lord will come. Why shouldn't we experience deliverance from the hand of death in the Name of Jesus? We need to understand there is an angel protecting each church represented by every reader of this book. We need to be clear of fussing and fighting against the leadership. If the leaders are maintaining their unity and we are living in harmony, we can become part of the solution. If we are, pray and release your angels to bless all your church, especially your leaders.

What kind of leader do you want to run your church? You would describe Jesus. What kind of husband or wife would you like? You would describe Jesus. That is why we get disappointed when leaders are not the same as Jesus. We do understand that they are imperfect. The Church is a supernatural body of believers. Live with this understanding, that every action, reaction, prayer, obedience, forgiveness will affect your church, and if you live with a kingdom, selfless mentality, your church will rule and govern the area where you live for the kingdom of God.

Pray These Prayers

We release blessing, Lord, to our leaders. To our pastors. To those in authority over us. We refuse to bind them. We refuse to stop the activity of our angels and the angel of the church. We refuse to disagree with the intercessory prayers of Jesus.

Let the Holy Spirit come upon you afresh, and begin to pray for your leaders with the Spirit of God. Take authority over anything that is coming against your leaders, their wives or their children. Take authority over it and release the angels. Let the angels work through your prayers now.

Holy Spirit, grip the people's heart with the intercessory prayers of Jesus. We confess Jesus as our Apostle and High Priest, our Advocate, our Defence Counsel. We rebuke accusation and condemnation. We refuse to be accused in the Name of Jesus. The accuser of the brethren has been cast down. We cast him down in the Name of Jesus. We command him to desist in his manoeuvres against our Church, in Jesus' Name!

Now consider our High Priest who has our name engraved upon the palms of His hands. He knows our name, the number of hairs upon our head. He knows all things about us and He still loves us. He knows the best and the worst, and He still loves us. Our name is still engraved upon the palms of His hands. He presents us to the Father because that is His ministry. That is His high-priestly ministry. He is our defence counsel: when everyone else may be accusing us, Jesus stands there as our defence counsel. He is praying for us, defending us and interceding for us according to the will of the Lord. Consider Him our Apostle. Consider Him our High Priest. Confess Him as such. This will release the angels to work on our behalf in every area of our life and ministry. God's word in our mouth will release the angels to act on our behalf. I want us to start to speak it out. Remember, the power of life or death is in the tongue. That is awesome. That means that life can be released through your tongue.

Let the intercessory prayers of Jesus grip you. We are going to speak words that will release our angels into our own situations. The Word of God shall not return empty but the angel shall go and accomplish the Word of God that we speak.

Let us send forth the Word of God and thank God that the angels are taking that Word and performing it. Be aware that angels are sent to do the will of God. Now receive the revelation afresh. I release it to you. I release increased activity of the angelic, into your life, into your family, and into your churches. There shall be an increased mobilization of the army, chariots and horsemen of the living God. It shall come to pass in your church and your situation. The angels shall cause growth, multiplication, deliverance and freedom.

5 The Rise and Fall of Lucifer

I was involved in drug abuse and occult study. I majored in astrology and studied all the numbers and signs and did charts for friends. One day I was approached by an evil angel who told me that he was one of the spirits that had the 'gift'. He told me that he would give me this 'gift' for a while. The 'gift' came and I was told about people, weird and wonderful things. I did a chart for someone's family and suddenly said, 'Your son will die.' I gave the time and place. When she phoned up and told me he had died exactly when and where I said, I didn't know what to say.

After two months (and I can still see the moment) this angel came back and asked, 'Do you want to get involved?'

I replied, 'NO!'

That was the end of it. I told my wife about what had happened and she asked, 'What was he like?'

I said, 'Beautiful.' I have not thought about it for twenty years, but I can remember he was beautiful; like crystal under a polarizing microscope, bright, precise and intricate. This happened before I came to know Jesus as my Saviour.

Peter Mourier

The archangel Lucifer was the choirmaster of heaven. Many believe one of his jobs was to be the praise leader of the heavenly hosts. All angels are beautiful, but Lucifer's beauty outshone them all. That is his past history. He still has the ability to masquerade as an angel of light, as an angel of beauty to deceive humankind. Lucifer has lost his original beauty and power and now all he exhibits is a charade. Many believe Satan (the word means 'no name') cannot create anything new and has copied God's order by setting up principalities, powers, thrones, might and dominion as a counterfeit.

The Bible narrates the rise and fall of Lucifer. 'The word of the LORD came to me: "Son of man, take up a lament concerning the king of Tyre and say to him: 'This is what the Sovereign LORD says' (Ezekiel 28:11–12). Many theologians believe that what followed was referring directly to Lucifer.

> You were the model of perfection, full of wisdom and perfect in beauty. You were in Eden, the garden of God; every precious stone adorned you: ruby, topaz and emerald, chrysolite, onyx and jasper, sapphire, turquoise and beryl. Your settings and mountings were made of gold; on the day you were created they were prepared. You were anointed as a guardian cherub, for so I ordained you. You were on the holy mount of God; you walked among the fiery stones. You were blameless in your ways from the day you were created till wickedness was found in you … Your heart became proud on account of your beauty, and you corrupted your wisdom because of your splendour. So I threw you to the earth; I made a spectacle of you before kings.
>
> (Ezekiel 28:15–17)

Francis Shaffer researched many civilizations and believed that their rise and fall followed a similar pattern to Lucifer's. At their beginning was a creativity which had the hallmark of God's creativity, and God allowed the superpowers to be raised up for a purpose: for example, the roads, trade routes and languages of the Roman and British Empires were used to spread the gospel message. Each civilization was destroyed after it became erotic, proud, perverted and self-centred.

On an individual level, very few people who have beauty, money and education will wholeheartedly submit their lives to Jesus. There are few nobles who have followed Jesus; most of us have come from brokenness, foolishness, rejected and despised backgrounds. God gave me a revelation to set certain things in order. He said to me, 'Son, you came to know Me because of your rejected condition. There are many people who don't know Me who have it all – a lovely family, swimming pool, education – but they do not know Me. You know Me because in the rejection and the pain you experienced, your search was born.' Most of us who have come to Christ have come like that. Have you ever noticed those who have beauty, position, money, education find it more difficult to surrender all and follow Christ? I have seen some with these talents come right through to Christ: there are some sold out for Christ, but there are not many.

Lucifer, the model of perfection, full of wisdom, perfect in beauty: he had it all. But then iniquity – wickedness – was found in him, and the sin of pride came into his existence.

Pride Precedes Lucifer's Demise

When God created angels, Lucifer was created as an archangel. It is thought that he was the chief angel. He was the most powerful and beautiful angel God created, but his beauty, wisdom and position went into pride. Lucifer then rebelled against God.

How you have fallen from heaven, O morning star, son of the dawn! You have been cast down to the earth, you who once laid low the nations! You said in your heart, 'I will ascend to heaven; I will raise my throne above the stars of God; I will sit enthroned on the mount of assembly, on the utmost heights of the sacred mountain. I will ascend

above the tops of the clouds; I will make myself like the Most High.
But you are brought down to the grave, to the depths of the pit.

Those who see you stare at you, they ponder your fate: 'Is this the
man who shook the earth and made kingdoms tremble, the man who
made the world a desert, who overthrew its cities and would not let
his captives go home?' All the kings of the nations lie in state, each in
his own tomb. But you are cast out of your tomb like a rejected branch;
you are covered with the slain.

(Isaiah 14:12-19)

Lucifer wanted to take the place of God and rule the universe.
Five times he says, 'I will': 'I will ascend to heaven; I will raise my
throne above the stars of God; I will sit enthroned on the mount
of assembly, on the utmost heights of the sacred mountain. I will
ascend above the tops of the clouds; I will make myself like the
Most High' (Isaiah 14:13–14). In other words, 'I will rule.'

If God had chosen to deal directly with Lucifer, He could
have destroyed him with a finger or a single breath. Instead, the
archangel Michael was sent.

And there was war in heaven. Michael and his angels fought against
the dragon, and the dragon and his angels fought back. But he was not
strong enough, and they lost their place in heaven. The great dragon
was hurled down – that ancient serpent called the devil, or Satan,
who leads the whole world astray. He was hurled to the earth, and his
angels with him.

(Revelation 12:7–9)

God told Michael to kick Lucifer out of heaven. Jesus spoke of
Lucifer – Satan – falling 'like lightning from heaven' (Luke 10:18).
That is fast!

Had God fought with Lucifer there would have been no contest. God is infinitely more powerful, and we need to remind ourselves that God's power remains greater than the devil's and the angels that rebelled with him. Angels have mighty power, but there is no duality between their power and God's power.

We need God to give us an understanding of His greatness rather than the greatness of Lucifer. Some look at what is happening on earth – death, sickness, injustice and adverse circumstances – and draw the wrong conclusion, that Lucifer must be powerful and God weak and ineffective. We have to be able to see God and Lucifer in the right way, lest we get too big a view of the devil. We need constantly to come back to the scriptures to get a clear view of the vastness of God and get a right perspective.

God's Winning Ways

A preacher had a recurring dream in which he was chased by two big lions. He tried to outrun them, but realized that they were going to outrun and overpower him. He was running with a friend but the lions caught the friend, overpowering and killing him. He thought, 'What must I do, as I can't outrun the lions?' He had a sense in his dream that he should face them and speak to them in the Name of Jesus. He commanded them in the Name of Jesus to stop and go – and they went.

He realized this was more than just a dream and had significance for his own ministry. He had a fear that needed to be faced. When he turned and faced the opposing lions and commanded them to stop in the Name of Jesus, he experienced a breakthrough in his own life and ministry. We need understanding and revelation to perceive correctly and to face and conquer our fears. The seeming contradictions will give way to the truth and we will walk in freedom.

Another preacher had a vision while he was preaching and saw a massive, fire-breathing dragon coming into his meeting. As this dragon breathed fire on him, he fell on his back to the floor. He saw Jesus standing with a drawn sword, and he cried out for help. Jesus just turned and looked at him, as if saying, 'You have got to do something about the devil yourself.' After a short time the preacher spoke the Word of God to the dragon. He said it was amazing: as soon as the Word of God touched the dragon, it began to go down like a hot-air balloon, right in front of him.

War in Heaven

> A great and wondrous sign appeared in heaven: a woman clothed with the sun, with the moon under her feet and a crown of twelve stars on her head ... Then another sign appeared in heaven: an enormous red dragon with seven heads and ten horns and seven crowns on his heads. His tail swept a third of the stars out of the sky and flung them to the earth. The dragon stood in front of the woman who was about to give birth, so that he might devour her child the moment it was born ... And there was war in heaven. Michael and his angels fought against the dragon, and the dragon and his angels fought back.
>
> (Revelation 12:1, 3–4, 7)

Let me tell you, if you have any dragons at home, get rid of them. Dragons have only one significance. If you have an elephant, it has significance, it is an animal from the earth. A dragon is only named in the Bible; the name belongs to Lucifer. So if you have anything to do with a dragon, I recommend that you get rid of it.

War broke out and the dragon and his angels fought. There was a great big cosmic battle. Lucifer did not prevail, nor was a place found for him in heaven any longer. The great dragon was cast out, that serpent of old called the devil and Satan, who deceives the whole world. He was cast to the earth and his angels were cast out with him.

> Then I heard a loud voice in heaven say: 'Now have come the salvation and the power and the kingdom of our God, and the authority of his Christ. For the accuser of our brothers, who accuses them before our God day and night, has been hurled down. They overcame him by the blood of the Lamb and by the word of their testimony; they did not love their lives so much as to shrink from death.

(Revelation 12:10–11)

The devil puffs himself up to look fierce and ferocious to bluff us that he has more power than he really has. God spoke to me once and told me, 'I have done everything, that I am ever going to do about the devil. I am not going to do any more. You have to do something with the authority that I have given you. Lucifer has already been defeated and dethroned.' Instead of him breathing fire and us lying down on our backs crying, 'Jesus, help me, take him away!', we need to rise up in the strength and grace of God and taking the sword of the Spirit to effectively pierce him. This will result in Satan being like a punctured hot-air balloon, deflated, defeated, deposed, fallen and paralysed. As James told the early Christians: 'Submit yourselves, then, to God. Resist the devil and he will flee from you' (James 4:7).

Our Position in Christ

We have seen that Lucifer – Satan – has been cast with his angels out of heaven. He is now prowling around seeking someone to devour. In Job, the first recorded book in the Bible, Satan went into the presence of God to ridicule and accuse Job before God. I have got good news for you. Satan, cannot go into heaven and accuse us any more because the accuser of the brethren has been cast down. Don't receive accusation from any source. God will correct us in His love, but He never accuses us. We are never to allow or permit accusation because we are 'in Christ', in the throne of God.

Don't ever say, 'I am coming into the presence of God.' A preacher once said that and the Lord asked, 'So where have you been all week?' We are the temple of the Holy Spirit and you could not live in God's presence any more than you do now. Jesus Christ, the hope of glory, lives in you. You are living in the holiest place, and the accuser of the brethren has been cast down. He is under your feet. Somebody once said, 'If you have a message for the devil, write it on the soles of your feet.' I have tried it and it works!

As a young Christian, I was once depressed, so I said to my pastor, 'I don't feel too good, pray and counsel me.' He did counsel me, but not in the way I expected: he said, 'Think that on one of your feet you have got "glory" written, and on the other, "hallelujah". Now, when you walk along, say, "Glory, hallelujah, glory, hallelujah". It's called the praise cure.' By the time I got back to my room I was praising God and the depression had gone.

In India I was preaching about our position in Christ: that Jesus is seated in the heavenly places on His throne and we are seated there too, with Him. The devil is under His feet and under ours, also. A man came up to me afterwards. His arm was stiff and he explained that a witch had cursed him.

'What can you do for me? Can you pray for me?' he asked.

He had listened to my preaching, so I asked him, 'Where is the devil?'

He said, 'He is under my feet.'

I then asked him, 'Can he be under your feet and on your arm at the same time?'

I saw him thinking, and then it seemed light and revelation burst forth into his mind and he said, 'No! Glory to God!' and he lifted his arm and wildly swung it around his head. He was gloriously healed right there!

When I read the scriptures, God often asks me, 'Are you going to believe your feelings or the scriptures?' I reply: 'I am going to believe the scriptures.' When I am feeling oppressed and it is almost as if the devil is squatting on my head, I read the scripture that says you are 'crowned with loving kindness and tender mercies'. I believe it, and in minutes, sometimes seconds, I am freed from all oppression.

It is a question of belief and perception. We can have such a big understanding of who the devil is that he alarms us and gets control of us, so we end up in complete deception. It has to do with the thoughts the devil puts into our minds, and nothing to do with the scriptures. When we return to the scriptures, we are walking in the truth again. Some people tell me the devil has given them a hard time and that he has been chasing them all week. I respond: 'Surely goodness and love shall follow me all the days of my life; and I will dwell in the house of the Lord for ever' (Psalm 23:6). It depends on what we see when we look over our shoulder. What is chasing us? The scripture says it is goodness and mercy that is chasing us. We have to stop and let the truth of the Word of God catch up with us.

Satan Down and Nearly Out

Lucifer has been thrown out of heaven and is down and out. A preacher from South Africa said that if he gets any trouble from the devil he calls all the evil host in. 'False prophet, you sit there. Antichrist, you sit there. The beast, you sit there.' He gets them sitting on the front pew and starts reading the book of Revelation to them. He said he has never needed to get beyond chapter 4 or 5 before they split. If you have problems with any demonic powers, just call them all in and say, 'Listen to this, to what the Bible says.'

Bob Gordon used the illustration of old-fashioned war. Stakes with sharp points were hammered into the ground, and when the horses and chariots ran towards them they were impaled on the stakes. He said the Word of God is like a stake pushed into the ground, sharp points placed all around you. The devil runs at you and he gets impaled on the Word of God. The Word of God is so powerful that it prevails every time.

'For … God did not spare angels when they sinned, but sent them to hell, putting them into gloomy dungeons to be held for judgment' (2 Peter 2:4). The devil is on a short lease, held by God for judgement, and I am looking forward to when the devil gets his 'just desserts'. I hate him for what he does to people, for his murder, lies, deception and his violence. I hate everything that he stands for and I am unashamedly glad that, as Jesus said, there is 'eternal fire prepared for the devil and his angels' (Matthew 25:41).

And the angels who did not keep their positions of authority but abandoned their own home – these he has kept in darkness, bound with everlasting chains for judgment on the great Day.

(Jude 1:6)

And I saw an angel coming down out of heaven, having the key to the Abyss and holding in his hand a great chain. He seized the dragon, that ancient serpent, who is the devil, or Satan, and bound him for a thousand years. He threw him into the Abyss, and locked and sealed it over him, to keep him from deceiving the nations any more until the thousand years were ended. After that, he must be set free for a short time ... When the thousand years are over, Satan will be released from his prison and will go out to deceive the nations in the four corners of the earth – Gog and Magog – to gather them for battle. In number they are like the sand on the seashore. They marched across the breadth of the earth and surrounded the camp of God's people, the city he loves. But fire came down from heaven and devoured them. And the devil, who deceived them, was thrown into the lake of burning sulphur, where the beast and the false prophet had been thrown. They will be tormented day and night for ever and ever.

(Revelation 20:1–3, 7–10)

They are to be tormented day and night for ever.

God's master plan for the devil when he fell to the earth was the cross. The cross was his undoing. 'And I will put enmity between you and the woman, and between your offspring and hers; he will crush your head, and you will strike his heel' (Genesis 3:15). This points to Jesus and the cross, which came thousands of years later. Jesus made a public show, an open spectacle of the devil, triumphing over him on the cross. The devil had no hope of winning, because Jesus came as the Saviour of the world. I am a saved person by the grace of God. I am not a sinner any more. We are the righteousness of Christ Jesus. Are your sins forgiven? Are you the righteousness of God in Christ Jesus? The word 'righteous' means blameless. 'God made him who had no sin to be sin for us, so that in him we might become the righteousness of God' (2 Corinthians 5:21). As Carmen sang, 'If the devil reminds you of your past, remind him of his future.'

God's Master Plan

God's master plan is the cross, and we got out of the hand of the enemy by being born again. 'For he has rescued us from the dominion of darkness and brought us into the kingdom of the Son he loves' (Colossians 1:13). We have been given a brand new nature, no longer a sin nature, but the nature and characteristics of the Lord Jesus Christ. Our spirit has been made holy and righteous, and so we have all the resources of God's kingdom and power, ours to fulfil the will of God and function with kingdom authority. Satan is no longer our father or king. We have been totally delivered from the devil's kingdom and placed in God's kingdom.

Some may need to have their minds and thinking renewed. There is no need to allow him to influence us in any way: we have been delivered from his hand completely. If your sins have been forgiven, give God the glory, and thank Jesus that 'In him we have redemption through his blood, the forgiveness of sins, in accordance with the riches of God's grace' (Ephesians 1:7). When we sin, it is foreign to our new nature, so we lose our peace and joy. When we repent, we get back to living in our proper lifestyle; in our new nature.

While in the USA I was driving on the wrong side of the road. My wife Joyce dug me in the ribs and said, 'You are not in England! Move back to the other side.' I quickly moved over, and it was good that I did because a few moments later a large lorry came rumbling round the corner. It was good to be on the correct side, but sometimes we go to the wrong side of the road. Our 'computer' has been programmed quite a bit by the old style, especially if we have come to Christ when we are older. So we have to de-programme it by the truth. Sometimes we find ourselves on the wrong side and need to say, 'Hey, what am I doing here? This is not my new nature, this is not the right side of the road for me. I need to move over on to God's side.'

Satan on the Prowl

You may never meet Satan personally, which is good news When it comes to some high-profile ministers who are doing big things for God, Satan will try to oppose them personally. For the rest of us, who are doing more minor things, he sends one of his agents, and so we should be careful about what we say. I have heard people say, 'I cast out the devil.' They didn't. They cast out one of his demons. Unlike God who can be everywhere, Satan can only be at one place at one time. If he is in another place, he cannot be with you where you are reading this book. Hallelujah!

David Yonggi Cho, a pastor from South Korea, once met Satan. He was in his hotel bedroom and was suddenly awakened to see Satan standing at the bottom of his bed. Satan tried to intimidate him, saying, 'I have come to kill you.' Cho was frozen with fear and could not speak. He knew the only answer to the devil was the Word of God, but nothing would come out of his mouth. Eventually, the Word of God flowed out of his mouth, 'For God did not give us a spirit of timidity, but a spirit of power, of love and of self-discipline' (2 Timothy 1:7). As soon as the Word of God came out of David's mouth, the devil stopped dead in his tracks. The devil told him, 'I am going now, but I will be back later to finish the job.' The devil is a liar and the father of lies: if he could have killed David Yonggi Cho he would have done it there and then.

Another apostle of faith, Smith Wigglesworth, was also woken up in the middle of the night and saw the devil at the bottom of his bed. But he said, 'Oh, it's only you,' and turned over and went back to sleep!

'Submit yourselves, then, to God. Resist the devil, and he will flee from you' (James 4:7). In the amplified version: 'Resist the devil and he must flee from you as in terror.' The devil is afraid of us because he is scared stiff of the Word of God, and the antidote to the devil is praise and worship. He is allergic to praise and worship. Use these two weapons, the Word of God and praise and worship, and the demons will have to flee from you.

God Gave You Feet

'Behold, I give you the authority to trample on serpents and scorpions, and over all the power of the enemy, and nothing shall by any means hurt you' (Luke 10:19, NKJ). A lot depends on what we believe about the scriptures as to how we will function. It will decide our fruitfulness: whether we are going to rise and succeed as God wants, or go along in a rut as Satan wants. Satan has fallen from heaven. Jesus says, 'Behold, I have given you authority.' That is the believer's authority, not only the pastor's or the minister's. Sometimes we lean too much on the ministry of one person, God wants to minister through His body, through every believer. I prophesy to you: in the revival that is coming to Great Britain, the two kingdoms will clash with increasing intensity. It will be the ordinary believers who will be doing the signs, wonders and miracles, as well as the five-fold ministers. The ministers will equip and release the saints to do the work of the ministry.

The work of the ministry includes miracles. It is abnormal Christianity when we do not see the supernatural. Signs, wonders, miracles, gifts of the spirit, salvation, healing, deliverance are all normal. Every believer reproducing: that is normal Christianity. In the revival, we will be seeing that. We will see boldness from the believers, a new breed preaching the gospel, going everywhere with signs and wonders, casting out the demons.

There will be tremendous clashes with the powers of darkness. Jesus said, 'I have given you authority.' There is no question about it. All we have to do is believe it!

The second part is this: 'To trample on serpents and scorpions' (Luke 10:19). I meditated on this verse, it is wonderful. Some people write it on the soles of their feet for the devil to read. That is the only place he can read it from, as he is under your feet. If you have a message for the devil, write it on the soles of your feet! God said to me, 'The busiest part of your anatomy should be your feet!' Why? Because the demon-infested world needs to be trampled on. 'I will give you every place where you set your foot, as I promised Moses' (Joshua 1:3).

This is the mandate that God has given: treading with authority the areas God has given us, we are sent out to tread down scorpions and serpents. We are to tread down the demons; we have a great ministry. We don't want to see the demons attacking our head; we don't see them in any other way except under our feet. 'To trample on serpents and scorpions, and over all the power of the enemy, and nothing shall by any means hurt you.' If we have been given authority by Jesus Himself over all the power of the enemy, is there any power left? As far as we are concerned the answer is no. As far as the Bible is concerned the answer is no. Jesus said, 'Nothing shall by any means hurt you.'

Over the years I have heard many statements that directly contradict this teaching by Jesus. We need to be challenged by something we may think or do. 'Well, brother, I am on the front line, therefore I am bound to be attacked by the devil,' we may think. We have opened ourselves to something with this statement! I am on the front line, walking in step with Jesus; I am in the blessed place. The ones who are opening themselves up to attack are the stragglers or the ones who run out in front, ahead of God. Sometimes my wife will challenge me, 'What are you expecting to happen? You are in the front line, in high-profile ministry – are you believing that the devil will attack you? You are in the front line – do not believe that you are bound to be attacked.' Wrong believing and the power of our words are opening up things of the demonic. If we expect it, the devil will make sure we get it!

A Truth Encounter

We do not need a power encounter to be delivered from the devil: we need an encounter with truth. The very moment we believe the truth of the Word of God, we are free – instantly. We do not need any great manifestations: just expect to walk out from oppression. Many that come to Christ do not have that understanding, and it is up to us to give it to them. It is up to us to give them the understanding of what has happened to the devil through the cross, what Jesus has done to him, his origins, his fall and the fact that every believer has authority over him.

God told one man, 'Tell the people to stop begging for more and start using what they have.' We have authority over the devil, but some of us are not using our authority. Some of us do not understand we have been given authority. You may have come from a background like mine, where you feel inferior. This is a mighty hurdle to overcome. It is amazing: as we begin to renew our mind with the Word of God and begin to understand who we are in Christ, we can walk anywhere and associate with anybody because of what God has done.

God asked me if I was scared of Him. My reply was, 'No!'

'Do you realize, son, that I have all the authority, wisdom and power? If I have it all, why are you scared of somebody who has only a little authority and power? I have placed you in My kingdom, as My son.' That set me free. The truth will always set us free. Christ is our deliverer!

The greatest deliverance from God happens when we are born again, when we are delivered out from Satan's kingdom and translated into a brand new kingdom. 'I have given you all authority.' A one-day-old Christian has been given authority if they would realize it. They can use and work that authority. 'I have given you authority.' Do you know that a one-day-old Christian is righteous before God, even though his performance is not yet sorted out, even before he is sanctified and cleansed? If this was not the case and he died that very night, where would he go to? He would go right into heaven, because of the blood of Jesus. The blood of Jesus gives us access into heaven. A one-day-old Christian has the right to go into heaven.

A one-day-old Christian has the right to deal with demonic powers. We make the demons too big in our thinking, we give them a different position to the one the Bible gives them. Instead of our going and trampling down snakes, scorpions and serpents for other people, we are having to do warfare continually for ourselves. This is not what God wants. God wants us to walk in the anointing, in the freedom, to believe the truth. We shall know the truth and the truth shall make us free. We will not be continually trying to cast devils out of ourselves or other believers. We will be walking in freedom with a renewed mind, declaring, 'I am seated with Christ and the devil is under my feet.' How can he be in our stomach and under our feet at the same time? Let's get real and begin to believe the Word.

Let's begin to deal with the devil and put him where he belongs, and then go and set the captives free. Our whole commission is to go and set the captives free. The captives are not the church people; they are world. That is where we are supposed to go, to the world. 'Go into all the world and preach the gospel to every creature.'

The devil does seek to cause sickness and disease. Sometimes we are too passive, and we receive things into our bodies that we should not receive. You are not sick and trying to get healed. You are healed – the devil is trying to make you sick. Your inheritance is health, and you have been given the authority to deal with sickness. While in India I ministered at a conference with about 600 people, 400 of whom got healed. All they did was to put their hand on the part that was afflicted and command the disease to leave. Tumours and cancers dropped off their bodies, incurable diseases were healed. If you are sick or oppressed, put your hand on your body and use your God-given authority. Command that mountain to move 'in the Name of Jesus'. Rebuke every work of the devil.

Jesus said, 'Nothing shall by any means harm you' (Luke 10: 19). If we have the concept that nothing is going to harm us, we can confidently go into the spiritual battle knowing we are not going to be wounded soldiers and end up in hospital. When we know our authority in Christ, we can go into battle treading down snakes and scorpions and all the power of the enemy, and nothing shall by any means hurt us. If this is what we believe and expect, this is what we will get. When you lead someone to Jesus, teach them this scripture. A new believer is not like a weak baby, fair game for the devil. Teach them this scripture and they can walk in freedom from day one.

God gave me this revelation: 'Son, you are seated with him at his right hand in the heavenly realms, far above all rule and authority, power and dominion, and every title that can be given, not only in the present age but also in the one to come' (Ephesians 1:20–21). If we believe that scripture alone, we will walk in total freedom from the devil's tyranny.

We have been deceived for too long: make a decision not to be deceived any longer. Lift your hands and say, 'Thank you, Lord, that I am free. Every oppression and every attempt on the enemy to deceive me is broken, in Jesus' Name. Devil, you are under my feet, I tread you down. I use my authority and I cast you out in the Name of Jesus. I declare I am free. I am seated with Christ in the heavenly places. I AM FREE!'

6 The Authority of The Believers

Demons Flee

When I was on a crusade in Singapore we encountered some tremendous opposition. We prepared for the crusade with a ten-day fast. It soon became apparent that we were up against demonic powers. Both of us became sick and I saw in a vision demonic spirits attacking us from an offshore island. My suspicion was a witchcraft coven, which was never proven but the crusade was littered with those witchcraft spirits.

On the first night I prayed for a youngish man who wanted to receive Christ as his Saviour. I discerned a witchcraft spirit was influencing his life and as I laid my hands upon his head and rebuked the evil spirit, he keeled backwards, spinning and manifesting demonic powers. It was not long before he was free. Most of the people who came forward needed a similar kind of deliverance. We had not encountered this before and so we began to understand why our fasting had been so tough. This boy's mother was a founder-member of the church, but she had taken him to the equivalent of a witch-doctor for a healing potion. This was why he needed deliverance.

On the second evening the mother responded to the altar call, expressing a desire to be baptized with the Holy Spirit. We later found out that she did not know Christ as her Saviour and that she was also full of bitterness. After the meeting I found her outside acting strangely. There is a monkey god that is worshipped in the east, and she was behaving like a monkey. For the next three nights, I tried everything I knew to set her free, but she became progressively worse. When we prayed, she became like a snake moving across the floor. On the second night a demon spoke out of her (I am not in the habit of holding conversations with a demon or even listening to them). The demon said, 'This is my house. I have been here a long time. This woman invited me here. If I go out, where can I go? You all have Jesus living in you.' The demon stubbornly refused to leave. I cried out to God for the key and He told me that she needed to repent. I talked, in her more lucid moments, about repentance.

On the third night she snaked across the floor again. In desperation I cried out to God: 'She is a founder member of this church, and this is the first charismatic meeting they have allowed. If she is left like this the charismatics will be blamed. Please do something to help us.' The lady snaked across the floor right up to the altar, then stood erect, picked up a golden cross and, lifting it high above her head, cried out, 'I want Jesus more than I want you, Satan.' She fell to the floor, instantly free from every demon.

She spent the next three days writing and telephoning everyone she had fallen out with to ask for forgiveness. We baptized a very Spirit-filled founder-member in the sea, alongside her son and a small group who had all given their lives to Christ. This has never been repeated in our ministry. We do know more now; this is not standard textbook stuff, it was a learning curve.

Can a Christian Have a Demon?

Our terminology is of the utmost importance here. Can a Christian be demon-possessed? A demon-possessed person is like the demoniac in Matthew 8:28–34; he is totally demon-possessed, body, soul and spirit. Consequently he is totally out of control, insane and unable to be subdued by men. The demoniac described in Matthew 8 was not a Christian and needed to be delivered from a legion of devils.

A Christian, however, has the Holy Spirit living inside and the human spirit has been recreated, regenerated. No evil spirit can cohabit with the Holy Spirit. Nevertheless, almost every believer accepts that Christians can be oppressed and demonized. Some say that a demon or demons can live in the body and wage war against the soul – emotions, will, mind – from this position. Others maintain that demons can be found in the soul of a Christian too.

Deliverance by Jesus

Let us look at the ministry of deliverance in the life of Jesus. He practised this often, with great results. His ministry focus was casting demons out of non-Christians, as there were no Christians around. If we believe the disciples became Christians when they initially followed Jesus our position changes slightly, but many will say that the definition of a Christian is for a person to have the Holy Spirit residing in them. Although the Holy Spirit rested upon the disciples, He did not come and live in them until the day of Pentecost. This is when many believe the disciples became Christians. Be that as it may, Jesus is never recorded as having practised deliverance on His disciples. He did, however, on the old covenant people of God, the Jews. 'And a woman was there who had been crippled by a spirit for eighteen years. She was bent over and could not straighten up at all. When Jesus saw her, he called her forward and said to her, "Woman, you are set free from your infirmity"' (Luke 13:11–12). Jesus cast out the evil spirit and delivered her.

There are those who practise deliverance on their church members or disciples. I knew a lady who still felt she had demons after being a Christian for thirty years. This dear saint received much deliverance but was still not set free. In these churches the same saints come week after week to be delivered of the same things. When I hear this, I have to conclude something is very wrong. If we are not free after thirty years with Jesus, or if we are going each week to be delivered of the same things, something is not working properly.

Let Righteousness Prevail

So can a Christian have a demon? A Christian can give place to a demon, but there is no need to do so. Christians have come to me for deliverance, but what they needed was to know the truth from God's Word. When they heard the truth, they walked in freedom. Others required repentance. If you are in a burning house, you do not need prayers of deliverance – you must run out. When a Christian is sleeping with prostitutes, he does not need a deliverance prayer. He needs to repent and then run out of the fire. Only then can he be truly free from sin and Satan, although he may still need to be cleaned up after his great escape.

There are three main categories of demonic influence in a person.

Oppression	This occurs from the outside and is a demonic attack.
Obsession	This is a demonic oppression that has now become a compulsion or perversion. An opening has been given for demonization of the mind and body. In this case, demons might have taken residence in the body or soul of a Christian.
Possession	Demons have taken over the spirit of a person and the demons are now in control. The person is often out of control.

I have known and dealt with both oppression and obsession among Christians, but a Christian cannot be possessed by evil spirits because the Christian is possessed by the Holy Spirit. As I have said, the Holy Spirit cannot cohabit with demons. When He moves in, they move out. 'Giving thanks to the Father, who has qualified you to share in the inheritance of the saints in the kingdom of light' (Colossians 1:12). Our human spirit is made righteous.

The only time a Christian could possibly become possessed would be if they renounced Christ, rejecting the truth by which they were once enlightened, and started actively opposing the truth or living a life that continuously defiles. Then, just as a conscious decision is made to follow Christ, so now a conscious decision is made to follow the demonic spirits. Judas was such: Satan had filled his heart.

Not every backslidden Christian is possessed, only those who by choice have ceased to be Christian and have turned their backs on Christ for ever. 'There is a sin that leads to death. I am not saying that he should pray about that' (1 John 5:16). John was writing about Christians and he was referring to spiritual death, eternal separation from a loving God.

Making Wrong Choices

I was able to encourage a backslidden Christian back to church. For over a year he again practised his restored faith. Then he fell away and returned to his old lifestyle, living as a practising homosexual. When I phoned or visited, he would be adamant that I should leave him alone. Each time I prayed for him he would start barking like a dog (a spirit of perversion). He is still practising homosexuality today. The apostle Paul puts it bluntly, 'those who live like this will not inherit the kingdom of God' (Galatians 5: 21). I pray that this man will return to Christ, but if he doesn't repent and return he will not enter heaven as a homosexual, regardless of current opinions. Like everyone else, he has to choose either to continue with Christ or to suffer the consequences. As Jesus warned, 'No one who puts his hand to the plough and looks back is fit for service in the kingdom of God' (Luke 9:62).

A minister's wife, a woman of great talent and beauty, was greatly used as a singer. A minister who was being taught by the Lord about demons and demonic possession saw this lady in a vision. He saw a demon sitting on her shoulder and whispering into her mind that with her beauty and great voice she would do much better singing in the world, where fame and wealth awaited her. She rejected these thoughts, and the demon left but returned and tried again to tempt her. Each time, the minister's wife refused and the demon left, until one day she began to listen.

In the vision the minister saw a black spot appear on the lady's head – her mind area. He realized that a demon was now controlling her mind with obsessive thoughts, but Jesus told the minister it was not too late; although she was obsessed, she could still do something about her condition. She was God's child and could return. At this point, if she had rebuked the demon she would have been released.

She continued to allow the thoughts in her mind, and it wasn't long before she left the ministry and went and sang in the world. Later, she left her husband and had a succession of unclean relationships with different men. The minister says he now saw the black spot go down into her heart area inside her (demonic possession). She completely turned her back on the Lord. God instructed the minister not to pray for her. She had committed the sin unto death.

'Ichabod, the glory has departed from Israel' (1 Samuel 4:21). This happened when Eli and his sons continually, day after day, week after week, month after month, year after year, lived in gross sin and wrongdoing. Eventually the ark of God was captured by the Philistines and taken from the temple. The glory departed.

The Holy Spirit will not cohabit with an evil spirit. When a person's continual behaviour makes it clear that they do not want the Holy Spirit in their temple, or spirit, and when a person chooses to follow and unite themselves with a demon, the glory will depart. 'Ichabod.' The Holy Spirit will leave.

Work out Your Salvation

Salvation is not based on a one-off decision. Jesus said to them all: 'If anyone would come after me, he must deny himself and take up his cross daily and follow me' (Luke 9:23). On another occasion He said: 'But whoever disowns me before men, I will disown him before my Father in heaven' (Matthew 10:33). Why are we exhorted by the apostle Paul: 'Continue to work out your salvation with fear and trembling' (Philippians 2:12)? He says this because salvation is an ongoing process. 'I give them eternal life, and they shall never perish; no one can snatch them out of my hand. My Father, who has given them to me, is greater than all; no one can snatch them out of my Father's hand' (John 10:28–9).

But we can choose to walk out of His hand ourselves. Far too many Christians are casual about their relationship with God. Carnality, compromise and sin abound on every side. Revival is coming. It is time to be serious and prepare for it. Our holy God requires us to live out our salvation. When we as Christians are walking in the 'fear of God', deliverance of demons from among Christians will become less and less necessary. We can then get on with the true deliverance ministry.

Be Faithful to the Word of God

Jesus and other ministers in the Bible moved in the power of God, which included the expulsion of demons. Study reveals that deliverance was performed on many. All of those who were delivered were non-Christians. In my latest shelf-search for a book on deliverance, I was amazed to find none on the subject.

Many years ago this subject material was on my shelf in abundance. If my memory serves me correctly the content was, 'How to do deliverance on Christians'.

The focus of Jesus and other ministers in the New Testament was to non-believers. Those who believe shall drive out demons. 'When the crowds heard Philip and saw the miraculous signs he did, they all paid close attention to what he said. With shrieks, evil spirits came out of many' (Acts 8:6–7). Philip was casting demons out of non-Christians and they left with great shrieks. Hallelujah! That is the kind of ministry to major in. That is the true ministry of deliverance. 'The seventy-two returned with joy and said, "Lord, even the demons submit to us in your name"' (Luke 10:17). Perhaps we need a 'How to do deliverance on non-Christians' book.

It is possible that we have been tricked yet again to focus in on ourselves instead of taking the message and the power of God out – hours, weeks, months (for some, years) that could have been spent on winning the lost and expelling demons from the mass of troubled humanity have been expended on casting demons out of the saints. Have we lacked wisdom? Have the ministers been worn out by this approach? The answer to these questions has to be yes. While every acknowledgement is made of some benefits (including to me) we will need to change and receive God's wisdom in this area for what lies ahead. The understanding I have gleaned about my position in Christ and walking in the truth of God's Word would have set me free all those years ago, as it does now.

Surely a fresh look, a wise approach is needed. The teaching of truth alone will set most Christians free. Shouldn't we major on that? To bring non-Christians to a proper new birth with true repentance and faith will stop us having to prop up premature babies for the next twenty years. Shouldn't we major on that? In revival, every dimension of God's kingdom is accelerated, including discipleship and deliverance.

Use Your Authority

While in West Malaysia at a packed church meeting, it was my privilege to witness the power of God through another preacher when a woman began to interrupt, crying out in a loud voice, 'This is a servant of God, who has come to show you the way of salvation. Don't be deceived, don't listen to him.' The speaker left the platform, went to the woman, who was not a Christian, and putting his hand on her head, he said, 'Keep quiet'. The lady crumpled on the floor, where she remained silently for the remainder of the service.

On his return to the platform, the speaker said to the people, 'The demons believe and tremble; but do you believe?' There was a holy hush. Our focus was truly on God. Needless to say, God moved powerfully in that service. It was an awesome sight to have witnessed this authority.

Those who practise deliverance on Christians should accept the challenge and take their ministry to the non-Christians. It may not be so 'safe' out there, but let us be radical. For those who do not practice deliverance, why not rise up, get out and get on with helping the unchurched? The masses are waiting for the gospel, with confirming signs of miracles, healings and deliverance. 'Then the disciples went out and preached everywhere, and the Lord worked with them and confirmed his word by the signs that accompanied it' (Mark 16:20).

There are those Christians who blame the devil for everything. If they sneeze, it is a demon that has just gone out! These folks do not need deliverance prayers: they need the truth, because they are deceived. If you see demons everywhere (although they are everywhere!) or if your focus is mostly on demons, you are in big trouble. This is the deception Satan loves because it puts him in control. The Bible tells us that we are to 'fix our eyes on Jesus' (Hebrews 12:2).

Use Our Weapons

'The weapons we fight with are not the weapons of the world. On the contrary, they have divine power to demolish strongholds' (2 Corinthians 10:4). This verse of Scripture was written to Christians. If every believer knew their weapons were mighty their lives would be different, but the staggering fact is most believers do not use their God-given authority. The strongholds mentioned here are not demons we must conquer in spiritual warfare, but strongholds of the mind, and we are to use our mighty weapons to pull them down and bring every thought into captivity to Christ.

Racism may be present in a Christian who doesn't even realize that it is there: it is called a blind spot. If you are a driver, you know blind spots can kill. Someone else will often see it and can reveal it to us if we are humble before God. The Holy Spirit will also often reveal these strongholds.

My own background was a socialist, working-class upbringing. In my mind a stronghold existed against those who had money and position. This racism was carried over into my Christian life. In Singapore some rich Christians loved our missionary team and showered gifts and treats on us. Our team had worked really hard for months, but instead of receiving this as a blessing from God, I became very angry. I reasoned that these rich Christians should give their money to the poor. I was like a toad, pouting, bristling with anger against these rich Christians. The still, small voice of the Holy Spirit spoke to me: 'Son, I have set this up to give you and the team a treat. Relax and enjoy it!'

I did obey the Lord, but the removal of this stronghold was a process. After many encounters with people and the Holy Spirit, a final breakthrough occurred.

In those days my wife and I were YWAMers (with Youth With A Mission). There was a professor on the staff, and for some strange inexplicable reason there were often negative reactions going on inside me against him. After I had prayed for wisdom, the Holy Spirit indicated that I should ask the professor to pray for me. After sharing my heart about my racist attitude, I asked this man to forgive me and pray for me. He graciously did so. I felt nothing, but as I lived out my Christian walk it was obvious to me that the stronghold had been totally broken.

If we are honest before God, and repent (change our mind), obeying the prompting of the Holy Spirit, either through other people or directly, we can see these strongholds of the mind destroyed. It is helpful at times to break the demonic element that is often imposed on an individual or a family. But once the strong man is bound, the freed person still must make the correct choices to walk in that freedom. Sometimes God works in us in an instant, and we are free, set at liberty 'to go and sin no more, lest a worse thing come on us'. We are able to build a new pattern in our lives, thereby establishing a stronghold for God.

God is just when He says 'love one another'; it would be totally unjust to ask us to do something we could not do. The same has to be true regarding forgiveness, or walking in joy. There have been certain days when I had a self-pity party – I wallowed in it. Sometimes this inward spiral took me into anger and depression, but God's Word came to me at these times: 'Seek first the kingdom of God and his righteousness and all these things will be added to you', or the words 'Rejoice in the Lord always and again I say, rejoice.' The choice was there before me. Most of the choices I made were to obey God's Word; once this choice was made God backed it up with the release of love or joy.

Fruit of the Spirit

The best weapon we have against our enemies is the fruit of the Holy Spirit. Human or demonic enemies can never fight or overcome genuine love. Christ's victory on the cross portrays the selfless love that conquered all the human and demonic powers in spectacular fashion. The fruit of the Holy Spirit released through the followers of Christ has the same profound effect. In my younger Christian years I was taught that the fruit of the Holy Spirit takes time to grow, in some cases a long time. How then do some very new Christians, who meet with God in a deep and radical way, flow at once with love, joy and peace, while some who are Christians for twenty years or more are still trying to cultivate this same fruit? It appears that the choice before all Christians is either to be controlled by the Holy Spirit and our recreated human spirit, or to be carnal, controlled by the fleshly selfish nature.

We have the ability to choose, to love, to rejoice, to be at peace, because God has put this wonderful fruit in our recreated human spirits. Don't wait for the fruit to grow: it's already within you waiting to be released. This doesn't mitigate against maturity, because the more we practise the more character we will develop.

We can build strongholds either for God or for our selfish nature. A stronghold of love will enable God to move powerfully through us to bring love to an unlovely world. God is love; those who choose to love live in God and God in them. 'Love keeps no record of wrongs' (1 Corinthians 13:5). Love does not keep a black filing cabinet, to store and bring to remembrance every wrong in the next squabble. We have to learn to live in God's love, a day at a time. Our past has been forgiven and forgotten by God for ever. His love keeps no record of wrongs and He commands us to love in a like manner. The devil can never overcome the fruit of love. He can only overcome us in the area of the selfish sinful nature; no wonder he wants us to build and reinforce the strongholds of the flesh.

However, we are to bring every thought into captivity to Christ. Sometimes this takes a bit of doing, because the Bible says they are strongholds. It is not a case of 'I need deliverance'. We have to learn to use our authority for ourselves against ourselves. Do not give in to these strongholds. Rise up and speak out with conviction to them. Address lust, prejudices, fears. Every stronghold has a breaking point. Persist until it is broken, and remember, the focus must return to the worship of Jesus. That is the key to staying free.

Stand for Truth

To digress for a moment, it is becoming increasingly common nowadays to say that we are what we are because of our genes and we have no choice in how we behave. It is said that a gay person is born that way; it is in their genes. The gay gospel robs those who believe it of personal choice. This minority group are very evangelistic in the propagation of the gay gospel. If you are born gay, why fight it, they say; instead, we will teach you to flow with your own sexual orientation. They are teaching that a lustful thought or action is not to be seen as a stronghold which needs to be demolished.

Something similar is said about alcoholics and thieves: it is in their genes. If it is to do with the genes, why lock up a thief when he steals? After all, it's not his fault! No, there are always consequences for our wrong consistent choices. The choices will, if consistently practised, produce strongholds in our lives, in our families and in our churches. We must be earnest, seriously prepared to deal with any strongholds, or, at a crucial time, at a point of victory, Satan will come and push our button in the area of that stronghold.

We may conclude that we need deliverance from evil spirits. Now this can be true, because the strongholds of the selfish nature will be reinforced by demonic activity, but the reason why the same folk come back week after week for deliverance prayers is because the strongholds have never been dealt with.

Be honest before God and pray actively against any strongholds; repent and forgive if appropriate. Make consistent choices to walk in the fruit of the Spirit; don't be tempted to excuse or justify yourself for not doing this. If you continue to struggle; share with another believer you can trust. Pray together to break the strongholds.

One of YWAM's main leaders shared how his Christian growth was almost non-existent for two full years after becoming a Christian. He then shared his struggles with a Christian friend. The two men became prayer partners. For the next six months the growth in his faith was almost unbelievable. This is a tried and proven key to growth and release. At certain times I have had to walk with the Lord and deal with strongholds alone – at other seasons, sharing with a trusted believer has brought a prayerful conclusion. Choose to flow and grow in the fruit of the Holy Spirit. If you do, others will be truly blessed by your gospel.

7 The Warrior

Bind a Demon

On a preaching trip to India I was taken to the village where we were to hold an evening evangelistic meeting. We were setting up our tent in the local square when I noticed, on one side of the square, a Hindu idol. I immediately sensed an evil presence, a demon. I realized to cast the demon out would not be helpful in the long term because the Hindu worshippers would encourage the demon to return with seven more. 'Then it goes and takes with it seven other spirits more wicked than itself, and they go in and live there. And the final condition of that man is worse than the first. That is how it will be with this wicked generation' (Matthew 12:45). I used my authority and commanded 'in the Name of Jesus' for the demon to be bound.

I went with the pastor and prayed with a number of believers in their homes before the meeting. As we walked from one home to another I received a vision of a demon bound from the ankles to the forehead in bandages, rendering it powerless to speak or use its hands. All this demon could do was jump up and down in rage, but it was impotent. The meeting took place and God's hand was upon it. The whole meeting flowed as God had free course. Praise God, He had the victory.

Rob Clement; West Sussex

A warrior is someone who fights and wins; a seasoned warrior has fought and won many battles. This is the call of God for us all: that we become warriors. No longer victims, but victors.

Warfare with Faith

Finally, be strong in the Lord and in his mighty power. Put on the full armour of God that you can take your stand against the devil's schemes. For our struggle is not against flesh and blood, but against the rulers, against the authorities, against the powers of this dark world and against the spiritual forces of evil in the heavenly realms. Therefore put on the full armour of God, so that when the day of evil comes, you may be able to stand your ground, and after you have done everything, to stand. Stand firm then, with the belt of truth buckled around your waist, with the breastplate of righteousness in place, and with your feet fitted with the readiness that comes from the gospel of peace. In addition to all this, take up the shield of faith, with which you can extinguish all the flaming arrows of the evil one. Take the helmet of salvation and the sword of the Spirit, which is the word of God. And pray in the Spirit on all occasions with all kinds of prayers and requests. With this in mind, be alert and always keep on praying for all the saints.

Pray also for me, that whenever I open my mouth, words may be given me so that I will fearlessly make known the mystery of the gospel, for which I am an ambassador in chains. Pray that I may declare it fearlessly, as I should.

(Ephesians 6:10–20)

We cannot conduct warfare without faith, but God is not going to ask us to do something that we cannot do. Some say they haven't got faith to fight the devil. Just do what God says and faith will be there when you need it. Paul asked prayer for boldness because he had known fear through his circumstances. His famous instruction from Ephesians 6 affords us insight into a realm of protection that many do not venture into.

Some have argued: do not take your armour off, but sleep with it on, then you will not need to dress again on rising. Surely Paul, the greatest warrior missionary (apart from Jesus) that has ever lived, would have urged us to do this in his writings if that was necessary, but he did not: instead he tells us we have to 'Put on the full armour of God'. As clever as these preachers sound, let us stay with the Word of God.

A plane can be airworthy, fully tested, checked and cleared for take-off. The pilot is not only guided by the assurance of another but has his own checklist, which he meticulously follows, step by step, check by check, until he is satisfied everything is in order and it is safe to fly. Have your own checklist. Be meticulous about the armour of God. Check it out, take it on, be totally prepared each day for the warfare you will definitely encounter. We are instructed to 'take off the old man, and put on the new man created in Christ Jesus'. This may puzzle you: you say, 'Wait a minute, I am redeemed, I am baptized into Christ, why should I "take off the old"?' Just do it. Obey and don't play mental gymnastics. 'Take off the old and put on the new' is what we are told to do in the Bible, and there is always a reason for everything written in the Word of God. Do it by faith, and you will notice the difference as you go through the day with fewer reactions and more godly responses in your relationships.

Get Properly Dressed!

How do you get dressed in God's armour? 'If you confess with your mouth, "Jesus is Lord," and believe in your heart that God raised him from the dead, you will be saved. For it is with your heart that you believe and are justified, and it is with your mouth that you confess and are saved' (Romans 10:9–10). There are two components here for salvation: heart belief and mouth confession. If you leave one aside, or favour one above the other, you will not enter the fullness of salvation. Some do not like to declare their faith but claim religion is a private affair. As we have seen, this is not what the Bible says, so we cannot negate the Word of God and make it of no effect. To be saved, we must declare, boldly and publicly, that Jesus is Lord.

A similar principle applies with the armour of God. Believe with your heart, as you dress up, that you are indeed clothed. Then confess with your mouth the reality of taking on Christ.

On many mornings, if you were in my room, you would hear me dressing up. I will say aloud to myself, 'I take on the helmet of salvation. "The LORD is my light and my salvation – whom shall I fear? The LORD is the stronghold of my life – of whom shall I be afraid?" (Psalm 27:1). I take on the breastplate of righteousness. "God made him who had no sin to be sin for us, so that in him we might become the righteousness of God" (2 Corinthians 5:21).'

Perhaps I should explain the word 'righteous': it means 'blameless'. We have right standing before Almighty God because of the holy, spotless, sinless blood of Christ. That blood makes us holy, righteous, blameless – appropriate it now! The foundation of God's throne is righteousness and justice; remember, God is blameless too. Don't be tempted to accuse or blame him for the evils of this fallen world.

Spiritual Check-up

A doctor was speeding and was stopped by the police. 'Oh, you are a doctor on call?' said the police officer.

'Yes, I am,' replied the doctor. The policeman let him off with a caution.

Many months later the doctor developed pains in the region of his heart. He was a Christian, and in a meeting went for prayer regarding these pains. The evangelist praying for him asked, 'Have you sinned in any way? Have you opened yourself to this attack?' He asked the doctor to check himself before God.

The doctor remembered the speeding incident. He had not been on call that night. After a sincere confession to God, the pain disappeared and has never returned.

Let us check that the armour is in place. God has provided it. He has done His part, let us make sure that we do ours.

'I now take on the belt of truth.' Jesus said that He was 'the way and the truth and the life' (John 14:6). Thank you, Lord, that the Holy Spirit is leading me today into all truth.

'I take on the gospel boots of peace.' Jesus said, 'I have given you authority to trample on snakes and scorpions and to over-come all the power of the enemy; nothing will harm you' (Luke 10:19). Thank you, Lord, for my boots. I tread down snakes, they are under my feet, I am walking victoriously. These gospel boots of peace are fitted to make us ready to preach the gospel of peace, so use them. Share your faith, be ready to witness. 'How beautiful on the mountains are the feet of those who bring good news, who proclaim peace, who bring good tidings, who proclaim salvation, who say to Zion, "Your God reigns!"' (Isaiah 52:7). You have been given the boots of peace, so put them on and bring peace wherever you go.

'I lift up the shield of faith.' We are exhorted to take up the shield of faith. I have done this and will continue to 'put on the full armour, and to take up the shield of faith.' Let me exhort you to do the same. It is for our benefit and protection. Tell yourself that you are now quenching all the flaming missiles of the enemy, and putting them out. Let this be especially true in relationships. We will often protect ourselves against overt attacks, but fail to keep the shield in place when covert attacks occur in friendships.

King David said, 'Even my close friend, whom I trusted, he who shared my bread, has lifted up his heel against me' (Psalm 41:9). David was gutted, wounded, cut to the quick. Guard yourself, take and keep your shield in place even in friendships.

'I take the sword of the Spirit.' This is the most awesome part of the weaponry. It is not defence, but attack. Jesus said to Satan, 'It is written,' and quoted scriptures that forced him to depart. You too need to quote appropriate scriptures as you dress, and you will be properly dressed for the war. You will be a protected person, ready for anything and everything.

Stand and Fight

My wife Joyce and I were standing at a bus station in West Malaysia, surrounded by the hustle and bustle of street traders and the constant clamour of people fighting for places on the buses. An Indian gentleman approached us with the offer to purchase lottery tickets. We politely declined his offer. Instead of moving away, he became more and more aggressive, until it became apparent he would strike out at me. I took a step back, alarmed and, I admit, a little afraid. I heard the words tumbling out of my mouth, 'I rebuke you, demons, in Jesus' Name.' The man's eyes went up into their sockets and started rolling, his body began to jerk and shake violently, and he was almost in a trance-like condition. Again I said, 'In the Name of Jesus, demons, go from this place.' There was now more urgency and authority in this statement. The man ran away, not only from us but right out of the bus station. We never saw him again.

We are at War

If we are to succeed, we need to understand that we are at war. The greatest weakness in spiritual warfare is that we don't know we are in it. Even some of us who know that forget it. We are not war-conscious.

Joyce and I went to Sri Lanka in 1983, just before the civil war broke out. My wife is originally from Sri Lanka and was walking down the road with an English friend. They were not thinking of guns and war, but were casually window-shopping. Suddenly a soldier pointed a gun at Joyce as if he was going to shoot her. Having just come from England, Joyce still did not think of war, and carried on walking. Her friend dragged her into the safety of a shop. Why was it that Joyce did not get out of the way? She was not war-conscious.

For the most part warfare is alien to us. 'One day humankind will learn war no more,' as one of the Old Testament prophets said. In other words, war is not natural to us; we have got to learn it. It is not natural to grapple with principalities and powers and overcome them. So we have to learn how to do it. We need to submit and surrender to the Word of God and learn that we are in a war. When some of us became Christians, we were told, 'Come to Jesus and you will know love, joy and peace.' That is only partly true. The other part is: 'Come to Jesus and you will know tribulation and warfare.' You are going to have to build some spiritual muscles and backbone. If you were a wimp with no backbone before you came to the Lord, you are soon going to be something to be reckoned with! God is going to train you to develop some faith muscles. You will start pushing the demons around and treading upon them. It is the way of the kingdom of God.

Sometimes people get a shock when they realize the magnitude of the warfare. Before, we were not conscious that there was a war. We just thought that things went wrong. We were not conscious that, when people hurt us or things went badly wrong, many of these occurrences were from the demonic realms – not all of them, but many of them. On becoming a Christian and walking in the supernatural realm with the Holy Spirit inside us, we begin to think in a different way.

The devil tries to oppose us. The Bible says that he is our adversary – he who stands against us, to hinder us. Because some new Christians are not warned about this they come to the conclusion that Christianity does not work. 'It is not the way they told me it would be.' Well, listen to me and I will tell you what it is going to be like. It is warfare. We are in a war zone, on red alert twenty-four hours a day. Isn't that good news! We need to recognize our war footing. The ministry of intercession and spiritual warfare in the Bible is not for a favoured few; we are all in the battle.

We had all better learn to intercede and do spiritual warfare, or we will become casualties. Each believer has been given authority over demons. Some have learned to use it; others have allowed it to be dormant, unused, but the authority is still given. You have more authority over your body, home and self than any person alive. You have more authority in your home than the pastor does. Did you know that? You and I must do our own warfare. We are all anointed to drive out evil spirits. The lie of the devil is that we are weak and that we cannot do anything about our circumstances or change what he is doing against us. That is a complete lie! The devil knows it, and we need to get the truth into our thinking.

Strength in Christ

'Be strong in the Lord and in his mighty power' (Ephesians 6:10). 'But I am hurt and confused,' you say. 'Give me some space and rest. Give me a day off, give me a break. I am going to take it easy for a while, I am going to duck and dive! It is too hot for me.

I will leave the devil alone if he leaves me alone.' There are a lot of Christians who feel like this – 'Devil, you leave me alone and I will leave you alone' – but there is no pact with the devil. We may not verbally say that or mean to do it, but this is how many people behave. The devil takes it seriously, because he knows that you have the potential to hurt him and his kingdom. In Christ we can do anything that God wants us to do.

Be Obedient

The famous missionary Hudson Taylor went to China without finishing his degree. That doesn't mean that all of us should stop studying and leave university! He was compelled to go; he had the call of God on his life. If you get to that point, you had better go. He went to China. He went by boat and the journey took about three months. We could be in China now in a matter of hours.

Hudson Taylor encountered tremendous opposition at the initial stages. He preached the gospel to those who had never heard the gospel before. The extensive work of the Overseas Missionary Fellowship (OMF), previously the China Inland Mission, began with that one man with the call of God on his life. Thousands have been led to the Lord because one man went. One man had the potential to change the course of history and the face of China. This is an incredible truth of the potential of one surrendered life. You, too, have tremendous potential. Will you surrender your life fully to God and obey His plan?

God has a plan for us – and the devil also has one, because he knows our potential. If we take God seriously and walk in His ways we can fulfil our destiny. But we must understand that when we make progress with God, the devil is going to oppose us. He has been studying human nature and human beings for a long time, and he will come to your weak areas and push the button where he knows that he had a reaction last time and got you to sin. He will use again the same area and compromise, the same circumstances, the same people. Even if you leave one group of people because you can't get on with them and go somewhere else, you may well find yourself in the same circumstances, because the truth is that running away solves nothing. Stand and fight, fulfil your call to overcome. 'To him who overcomes, I will give the right to sit with me on my throne, just as I overcame and sat down with my Father on his throne' (Revelation 3:21).

Victory Guaranteed

Victory is guaranteed, and that is why we are called to be Overcomers. We are called to do something about what the devil seeks to do in our lives. We can tell the devil, 'You are not pushing that button again. It is not going to work this time.' That is the way to overcome. The devil knows your potential even more than you, so ask God to give you a revelation of your potential, of what He can do through you if you consecrate, set apart, your life for Him. God will shake the powers of darkness and do great things through our availability. Yes, we may sin, but we receive mercy and grace when we fall. Mercy forgives and restores us, grace enables us not to repeat the sin. Grace is God's divine enablement to overcome.

Know Your Enemy

'For our struggle is not against flesh and blood, but against the rulers, against the authorities, against the powers of this dark world and against the spiritual forces of evil in the heavenly realms' (Ephesians 6:12). How many of you have had a fight in relationships against flesh and blood? Most of us have become skilled in fighting people. But when we come into the kingdom of God, we are told not to fight for our rights, not to fight people.

We have an advocate with the Father. We have a new standing. We do not have to demand our rights. God makes sure that we get what we need, because God looks after His children. Now we have to learn how to conduct spiritual warfare and fight against wicked spirits and powers of darkness, to turn our cannon against the demons instead of the people.

In my long distant past, I had numerous drinking bouts and sometimes fights with my brother-in-law. Many years later, after becoming a Christian, I was travelling on the Underground in London and I bumped into my now ex-brother-in-law. We were genuinely happy to see each other after so long, but he looked in terrible shape. Age and constant abuse of alcohol had taken its toll.

Many hours were fruitfully spent with me telling him how I had received Christ as my Saviour since the last time we had met. He was taken aback. He was stunned by the change he saw in me, and interested to know more. His girlfriend accepted Christ later that day, much to my delight – and his annoyance! Over the next months I had further opportunities to share the love of God with him.

One day I caught him kissing a 15-year-old girl whom Joyce and I were caring for. I stopped him and he walked off in a huff. The next day he returned, drunk, drugged, foaming from the mouth, and wanting to fight me. Quietly I said, 'In the Name of Jesus, Satan, I rebuke you.' The discernment of spirits started to operate and I watched as a demon went out of his feet and left him. I added: 'Jack, I don't fight nowadays. I love you. If you hit me, I will not hit you back.'

He became very meek and lowered his fist, and I asked him into the house for a cup of tea. As we sat drinking the tea, we talked about repentance and faith in Christ. He was truly a lost man, but nevertheless interested.

Demons can be cast out of non-Christians. Sometimes we don't use our God-given authority, and can suffer unnecessarily.

Watch Out!

We will never build good relationships by fighting people. Contention breeds more contention and the only way out of that syndrome is to repent, say sorry and be reconciled. For instance, you can be in a planning meeting, not agreeing with the other people there. The devil doesn't like plans for the kingdom of God and so he will try to exploit the disagreement to make you end up fighting. It is a good strategy to pray before such strategic planning meetings, deal with the enemy, fight against his interference, spoil his tactics and enjoy a good kingdom meeting!

We need to create a faith-filled environment for our relationships and command the enemy to desist in his manoeuvres against us. Then peace will come. Learn to recognize the footprints of the devil, and then go after him rather than after the offending person. As we do spiritual warfare, we must use the Name and the blood of Jesus and become skilled in the use of God's word against the enemy.

There are certain people who often cause me a lot of hassle. Now, before I visit them, I bind demonic powers. Then everything is rosy! It will work for you and it can work in every situation. Remember, you are in a war zone. If you forget, you will get caught off guard, and the enemy's missiles, instead of getting extinguished on the shield of faith, will pierce and wound you. Be alert and keep your shield up.

One Christmas one of my relatives verbally attacked me. I was not alert and did not have my shield in place, and returned home spiritually wounded and bleeding. It took weeks to fully recover. The Lord comforted me and healed me, and I repented of my anger. I felt I wanted to pick my relative up and give him a little shake – have five minutes off from the Lord and then repent afterwards! Now at Christmas I'm on red alert – an increase of prayer, weapons at the ready – to bless the people. Being beaten up once is enough. Spiritual warfare works, but not always in five minutes. It can be a dangerous time: it is easy to take a break from God, chill out and pig out – food, old films, sleep and backsliding. If you are visiting home or family, do not just relax: remember, you are still involved in the spiritual battle and the devil has not taken a holiday.

Strength in Unity

There are two main reasons why it is important to keep our relationships with other people right, especially with other Christians. We have had the gospel for a long time, but the world has not been reached. Why? The church down the road is fighting the church down the next street. The leaders are fighting other leaders. There is strength in unity.

When birds fly and migrate they fly in a 'V' formation. The flock get where they are going because they have this 'V' formation. The bird in front stays there for a while, then swaps over with another bird. He takes the full force of the wind that is against them all, and the others tuck in behind him and get a free ride. In this way they can travel thousands of miles, and they do together what they could never do by themselves. This is why the Lord Jesus prayed for unity in the Church (John 17:11–23), so that we can evangelize the world and get the job done.

Watch and Pray

Two years ago, I was awoken in the early hours of the morning. I had been having a dream in which I saw my pastor and his wife, and an aeroplane completely surrounded by angels. The angels were not only holding the plane up but moving it in the air. On waking, I knew that I had to pray for the safety of my pastor and his wife, as they were on an aeroplane to South Africa. I continued for over an hour, crying out to the Lord, knowing that His hand was on the plane and His angels were around it, protecting and guarding His children. A few days later, I heard that the plane had needed to make two unscheduled landings as there had been problems with the flaps, but the plane had arrived safely in South Africa.

Bev Clement; West Sussex

Through intercessory prayer we become warriors. Through prayer the Holy Spirit will deal with the most stubborn heart and bring conviction of sin. For most of us, if not all of us, someone prayed for our conversion. I used to play football with a young man – I didn't even know that he was a Christian. After I became a Christian, he told me that he had been praying for me. I praise God for such people. We often pray and ask God to give people a spirit of wisdom and understanding, allowing them to see themselves from God's perspective. That is a godly way to pray.

If you are an intercessor you may not be the one who is seen up front. However, some of the revivalists had intercessors who would spend weeks on their knees in prayer, and they would pray until the breakthrough came. When the revivalist Charles Finny preached, it is said that 80 per cent of his converts stayed converted. Compare that with the modern-day preachers, who have 10 per cent of their converts go on. One of the reasons is the lack of intercessory prayer today. When the rewards of heaven are given out, who is going to get them? I tell you, the intercessor is going to be right up at the front with Jesus. Our highest call as a people of God is to pray, and the highest call is to be a prayer warrior.

8 The Warrior's Winning Ways

Witchcraft to Christ

In West Malaysia, a famous medium was saved and he invited us to come to his town, to preach the gospel to a large Buddhist family. Our group prayed and cried before God for souls to be saved. It was a powerful prayer meeting and we knew something dramatic was about to unfold. The kingdom of God had been loosed and the demonic powers bound. We were ushered into a massive house where at least thirty people had gathered. Dominating the room we were in was a huge altar loaded with fruits and drinks, offerings to the deity. Along the altar was a line of brightly lit candles and the sweet smell of incense permeated the whole house.

After I had preached and testified, sixteen members of the family and their friends knelt to receive Jesus as their Saviour. No sooner had they prayed than a wind blew into the house and extinguished the lit candles. All present took it as a sign from God that the demons had been bound and the captives set free, and we rejoiced late into the night over the victory God had won.

Free Salvation

The apostle Paul told the Ephesian Christians, '[God] raised [Jesus] from the dead and seated him at his right hand in the heavenly realms' (Ephesians 1:20). Jesus is seated in heaven because the work that He came to earth to do is finished. We overcome the devil not by the works we do, but by Jesus' finished work of Calvary. On the cross Jesus cried out, '"It is finished." With that, he bowed his head and gave up his spirit' (John 19:30).

We cannot earn our salvation, it is by faith in Christ alone. When we come to Calvary by faith and receive what Jesus has done for us, when we know that God has forgiven our sins and that we are his children, this will change us on the inside.

We will not be bowed down with condemnation, saying we are sinners, no good, useless and never going to amount to anything. If you think like that, the nagging voice in your mind is the devil, the accuser. Kick out those accusations, and stand tall!

'For we are His workmanship, created in Christ Jesus for good works, which God prepared beforehand that we should walk in them' (Ephesians 2: 10, NKJ).

Now we begin to walk differently as we have a sure step. We walk with confidence and boldness. Is it wrong for us to say, 'I am strong in the Lord and in the power of His might'? No, we need to know who we are in Christ so that we can overcome the devil. If we keep saying we are weak, an emotional cripple, people may start to agree with us. Yet those who are mature in Christ will see the true potential in us. They will speak and call it forth, speaking words of faith. They are the people to be around rather than those who only speak negatively. God sees us as we really are – perfect, because of the finished work of Calvary.

Seated with Christ

Paul went on to tell the Christians in Ephesus: 'And God raised us up with Christ and seated us with him in the heavenly realms in Christ Jesus' (Ephesians 2:6). We have to learn to sit down and rest in our faith; to relax in the presence of God, trusting in His promises. Put the promises of God around your waist and hang loose, with the Word doing the work! Enter into the Sabbath rest of God. We can walk with confidence and boldness, making a deliberate choice daily to take off the 'old man and put on the new man'.

'Put off your old self, which is being corrupted by its deceitful desires ... and put on the new self, created to be like God in true righteousness and holiness' (Ephesians 4:22,24). Talking off the old and walking in the new, or walking in the Spirit, is a decision that we have to make every day of our lives, and is a very practical matter.

Let me give a few examples. 'Do not let the sun go down while you are still angry' (Ephesians 4:26): if you go to bed angry, you will wake up in the morning oppressed by the devil, as you will have given him a foothold – sort it out before you sleep. 'Pride goes before destruction, a haughty spirit before a fall' (Proverbs 16:18): pride is an attitude of heart. We have to make choices to humble ourselves. A man recently told me he had made a mistake and asked for my forgiveness. I had never heard that person do that before. Usually he shifted the blame to someone else and tried to justify himself, but the fact that instead he asked for forgiveness was a sign of maturity, of a person growing in Christ. If we do something wrong we have to own up and take responsibility. That is humility. If you are ever tempted to shift the blame to others and defend yourself, especially out of insecurity, stop for a moment, and either say nothing or ask for forgiveness. In any situation we can react in the flesh, the old man, or in the Spirit, the new man.

Right Balance

When I was a young Christian I was very zealous; not much wisdom but a lot of zeal!. I was out on the streets of Brixton,

London, preaching over the noise of the traffic. The group I was with were zealous, but they began to follow the teaching of a certain Bible teacher. They started out right, but went off on a tangent. He was saying, 'I am right and the others are wrong.' They became an exclusive group and began to do everything he taught them. God got me out of it, but we need to beware of extremes because this is one of the ways the devil uses to spoil a Christian's usefulness. Most of the water has returned to the river's flow, but a few stagnant pools are left. In restoration of truth and new moves of God, enter into all that God is doing, but seek wisdom from God, to avoid extremes.

We must have balance, and nowhere is balance needed more than in the matter of Christians and demons. As a young Christian, I was casting demons out of Christians. Then I read a book that said a Christian cannot have a devil, and so I went from one extreme to another. I am now convinced that no born-again Christian can be possessed.

While visiting a hospital I led a dying Buddhist man to faith in Christ. As I was praying for this man to be healed, the Lord spoke to me: 'Cast that evil spirit out of him.'

I protested, 'Lord, he is a Christian now, he cannot have a demon.'

The Lord repeated the instruction. Edward, my brother-in-law, was praying with me. He knew nothing of what God was telling me to do, but he turned to me and said, 'God says you are to be obedient. Do what He is telling you.'

I said silently, 'Lord, I don't believe this, but I am going to do it anyway.' I prayed against the evil spirit and cast it out of the man, who then manifested and the demonic spirit went out of him.

He turned and looked at me and said: 'Thank you. That is marvellous – I am free at last.' So my theology changed again!

I find it hard to understand how some people can insist that demons do not exist or that no Christian can be demonized when they have been having nightmares for fifty years. After the spirit has been rebuked, they sleep like a baby, never to have nightmares again. Surely they have been delivered.

'A false balance and unrighteous dealings are extremely offensive and shamefully sinful to the Lord, but a just weight is His delight' (Proverbs 11:1, AMP). The other extreme is the teaching that every Christian has at least one demon, and this is certainly an abomination to God.

The biggest deliverance occurs when we become Christians; we are delivered from the kingdom of Satan's darkness and translated into the kingdom of light. The church where I was born again in March 1973 was brilliant – a fiery pastor and many aspects of a loving family. Yet while many dynamic truths were shared and learned, we did not know the full abundant, overflowing truth of the word 'salvation'. I was soundly 'saved and filled with the Holy Spirit and speaking in other tongues'. My pre-Christian involvement with the occult gave rise to oppression and depression. This part of salvation was not adequately taught or dealt with. There were days of internal civil war going on, and the many biblical truths that I was learning did not seem to help in this area. I was desperate for relief. What I needed, but I did not know it at the time, was deliverance from demons.

One day the Holy Spirit revealed, 'David, you are seated with Christ in heavenly places. Satan and the demons are under your feet' (Ephesians 2:6,17–18). I walked in this truth for a day, and the freedom was beautiful. This was the days before the 'In Christ Jesus' teaching. (The author refers to this in more detail in Chapter Two, 'Our Full Salvation'. See also *In Christ Jesus*, Colin Urquhart, Kingdom Faith Ministries, 1997.) The following day was dark and oppressive. I had allowed the fleeting revelation to slip out of my heart. With only this scripture I could have walked in freedom. It is possible to walk free from demonic oppression from day one of salvation if the truth is understood and believed.

True Freedom

After two years of this internal tug of war, God answered my prayers. A lady in the church advised me to visit two Anglicans, Captain Jimmy and Fyvola James, who were laid-back, middle-class Anglicans. They were polite and loving, but the ministry they were engaged in was anything but laid-back. They told me that I needed to be set free from the occult involvement of the past. Scripture references from the Old and New Testaments established the need for repentance and faith, because without a true repentance full deliverance is impossible to maintain: Jesus said, 'Be healed, now go and sin nor more lest a worse thing come to you.'

A time for good preparation was agreed. The next few weeks were to prove a turning point in my life. After repentance and renunciation, strong prayers of command were made by the Jameses on my behalf. We had at least three sessions over the next four weeks. On the way to the first prayer session, fear hit me in the pit of my stomach. I was on the point of not going, but by an act of will I decided that I would go. Past involvement in the occult was about to be addressed and broken: spiritualism, rosicrucianism (three years' involvement), palmistry, numerology, astrology, astral travelling, to name just a few. As the Jameses prayed, the inner tension mounted to breaking point, and demons choked and gagged out of my mouth. The experience was awful, and the fight intense.

Each session left me feeling lighter and freer. When the hours of prayer were finally over, the inner fight ceased. The warfare continued, but not like before; now it was outside, not inside, so it was easier to deal with.

Now I know that in some circles this is controversial. I was not possessed – my faculties were in place. I was not mad, but I was demonized. My salvation was assured: my spirit was possessed by the Holy Spirit, not demon spirits. The truth of God's Word could have set me free if I had held it at the beginning. Many Christians today are sick, oppressed and down and out of the fight. It is not all demons, but much of it is.

My left eye sees very little; it runs in my family, an inheritance from the Lambs. Others have the same problem. Now, with the new inheritance I have in Christ, I am free from the old inheritance of sin, but I have to appropriate it by faith At times the truth has directly set me free; at other times the truth in which others walk has, through their faith, enabled me to receive the help, aid and assistance needed.

Potential Waiting to be Released

There is the potential for a newly born-again Christian to be delivered from every demon at the time of salvation. In revivals, sinners meet with God at such a deep level that true repentance and faith in God takes place. A powerful witch-doctor who gave his life to the Lord commanded his own demons to leave, and he was instantly delivered. Others who receive and follow Christ have been baptized in the Holy Spirit and water at the same time and on the same day! The potential is there, but so many who come to Christ have done it in an incomplete way. The teaching they have received may have been only partial – and they receive only partial freedom and partial deliverance.

Some Christians, every time the pot boils over, the door slams, the car radiator steams, say it is the devil! Some of you may have been there – 'The devil is attacking me!' One man came for counselling because the door was squeaking: oil solved it. Another woman came because she had a pain in her leg: the strap of her shoe was too tight, and so we asked her to throw away the shoes. She was instantly cured!

The devil is quite happy to get the blame as he gets centre-stage, and incidentally this is a danger to which intercessors must be on their guard. We teach those involved in intercession to serve in practical ways, as this helps them to keep a proper balance. By all means be informed and aware of the enemy, but be impressed with God. Don't be impressed with the devil and only informed about God. The devil seeks to impress us and to puff himself up and tell us he is in control, but he isn't. We live in a fallen world, and if the pot boils over or I put the car in an unlawful place and get a parking ticket it's my own fault. We cannot blame the devil for everything.

We also need to recognize that, in some instances, it is God who is dealing with things in our hearts and lives, pruning, disciplining and correcting us. It is not the devil, although some of us have blamed him for what is happening. Next time you feel uncomfortable and under pressure, do not automatically say it is the devil. It could be God, putting fire into your life to bring impurities to the surface so they can be purged out.

Deliverance Ministry

When I was a young Christian I was into heavy-duty deliverance sessions. I would be involved night after night casting out evil spirits. It was a life of oppression and exhaustion. My wife Joyce knew we didn't have it right and that something was wrong. She would ask, 'Are you sure about this? Have we really got it right?' I would say, 'Of course we have. We have all these people lining up.

We have a great deliverance ministry!' Christians flocked to us, and we got exhausted. I wish I had listened to her, but God had to sort me out through many hard trials.

Some people who have 'deliverance ministries' do not teach the people how to stay free, but they teach them to be dependent on them. They may have the gifts and calling, but an insecure minister may keep a person coming back again and again to them, as this makes them feel useful. But what they are doing is only feeding their insecurity.

The devil will also try to get you into areas of pride. 'I have a great deliverance ministry.' You will come down with a big bump if you believe that! I have heard people say, 'My ministry is a deliverance ministry,' but this is going off at a tangent. There is nothing in the Bible that talks about a deliverance ministry. If you are pastoring, loving people and witnessing to the lost, that is a great balance. If your focus is on one thing you will go wrong. You must learn to focus on things that are important to God.

Do not misunderstand me. Deliverance is real, but what do you do when somebody needs to be set free? Set them free, pray for them and then move on. Some people want to be in the limelight even in deliverance sessions. One night, a young man who had just seen a film called *The Exorcist* called me out to pray for him. He was not a Christian, and the Lord told me he was just putting on a show. He had crushed some Christmas decorations and blood was all over the place. He was rolling around and screaming on the floor, but he was doing just what he had seen in the film. I said 'Stop that!' and made him sit on the chair. He did exactly what he was told. The young man was wonderfully born again a few days later, and became a youth leader. He returned one day to thank me. Be careful that people do not manifest and roll on the floor just to be in the centre of the limelight. That is what the devil wants – to be centre-stage and to push Jesus into the wings.

Stay Free

If you want to be delivered and set free, you cannot stay centre-stage; that place is reserved for Jesus. We must ensure that the people we minister to know the true gospel, repent and receive Jesus Christ into their lives, or we will waste precious valuable hours without fruit.

There are people who are still seeking deliverance from demons after years and years of walking with Jesus. I do not judge them, but I feel for them – saved, but not knowing the fullness of salvation. We must instruct people how to keep their freedom and walk in it so that they do not become dependent upon us, but upon the Lord.

A young lady received prayer for demonic oppression. Her freedom was instant, but she returned some weeks later with the same oppression. She was taught about the blood of Christ and how to use the Name of Jesus against the demons. The young lady prayed for herself and was again instantly released. She did not return, because she knew how to stay free herself.

I understand the need for believers to be helped in the area of demonic oppression. There are some reasons for oppression among Christians. For each of these reasons there is also an antidote.

Reason: Unforgiveness (number one area of oppression)
Antidote: *Forgive those who sin against you or hurt you.*

Reason: A lack of clear understanding regarding the truth of
            God's Word

Antidote: *Walking in the truth – that is the biggest deliverance we will ever experience.*

Reason: Deception, actively believing the lies of demons
Antidote: *Receiving help and submitting to godly leadership.*

Reason: Refusal to be rooted in a live church (exceptions being: no live church around, or shut in by illness or age)
Antidote: *Obey Jesus and root yourself in a live church.*

Reason: Opposition to the leadership of God's anointed leaders
Antidote: *Repent, 'fear God' and touch not His anointed.*

Reason: A lifestyle of sin
Antidote: *Repent, and believe. Repentance is ongoing. Keep short account with God daily.*

Reason: Incomplete birthing, no true repentance for salvation
Antidote: *We have to make sure that we present the full gospel and see that there is true repentance.*

Reason: Christian by name but not by experience
Antidote: *Meet with God and be born again.*

Depression is a major way in which the devil seeks to oppress Christians. I recommend you do what I do: I refuse depression. I won't have it! Depression sometimes comes to people and they do not recognize that it is from the devil. The devil will bring depression and accusation. He will start accusing you in your mind and making you depressed in your emotions. You have to refuse what the devil tries to put on you. Once the devil knows that you know what he is trying to do and that you believe you have authority over him, he will flee from you and the depression will lift.

Some people say, 'Keep your eyes on Jesus,' that is all you need to do. Yes, we must do this, but we must also recognize the devil's tactics. If we don't do this, how are we going to outmanoeuvre his strategies and the things he is seeking to do against us? During a battle, you look at the commander but you are also looking at the enemy. You have to do both. While we look at the enemy, we need to be constantly aware of the presence of God. We know that 'if God be for us who can be against us?', we are more than a conqueror in any battle, but at the same time we see the footprints and hallmarks of what the devil is trying to do. Then we recognize him and enforce Calvary's victory over him, which leads us to the real source of how we can be victorious warriors: the death and shed blood of the Lord Jesus Christ.

The Blood Speaks

'To Jesus the mediator of a new covenant, and to the sprinkled blood that speaks a better word than the blood of Abel' (Hebrews 12:24). How can the blood of Christ, who died two thousand years ago, be relevant in the new millennium?

> *Now Cain said to his brother Abel, 'Let's go out to the field.' And while they were in the field, Cain attacked his brother Abel and killed him.*
>
> *Then the LORD said to Cain, 'Where is your brother Abel?'*
>
> *'I don't know,' he replied. 'Am I my brother's keeper?'*
>
> *The LORD said, 'What have you done? Listen! Your brother's blood cries out to me from the ground.'*
>
> (Genesis 4:8–10)

The blood of righteous Abel was speaking out for vengeance. Cain received a curse on his life in judgement for his brother's murder. The blood of sprinkling speaks a better word than that of Abel. Abel's blood is crying out from the ground for vengeance; the blood spilled on the cross of Calvary is crying out, not for vengeance, but for our forgiveness.

The blood from the nails in the hands and the feet of Christ is speaking. The Father is listening and is totally satisfied with the blood of Christ. God is not counting man's sins against us any longer. How can that be possible? It is because of the blood. All those who truly repent and believe that Christ died and shed His blood will be forgiven of all their sins.

Here are some of the 'better things' that the blood of Christ is speaking:

- *The forgiveness and cleansing of sins* 'If we confess our sins, he is faithful and just and will forgive us our sins and purify us from all unrighteousness' (1 John 1:9).
- *The removal of every curse* 'Christ redeemed us from the curse of the law by becoming a curse for us, for it is written: "Cursed is everyone who is hung on a tree"' (Galatians 3:13).
- *The healing of our bodies* 'He himself bore our sins in his body on the tree, so that we might die to sins and live for righteousness; by his wounds [blood] you have been healed' (1 Peter 2:24).
- *Bold access into God's throne-room* 'Therefore, brothers, since we have confidence to enter the Most Holy Place by the blood of Jesus, by a new and living way opened for us through the curtain, that is, his body' (Hebrews 10:19–20).
- *The overcoming of Satanic and demonic powers* 'They overcame him by the blood of the Lamb and by the word of their testimony;

they did not love their lives so much as to shrink from death'
(Revelation 12:11).

- *A clear conscience* 'How much more, then, will the blood of
Christ, who through the eternal Spirit offered himself unblem-
ished to God, cleanse our consciences from acts that lead to
death, so that we may serve the living God!' (Hebrews 9:14).
- *Removal of God's anger* 'Since we have now been justified by
his blood, how much more shall we be saved from God's wrath
through him!' (Romans 5:9).

To appropriate what God has accomplished for us, we must
believe and have faith, but there is a further step. 'They overcame
him by the blood of the Lamb and by the word of their testimony'
(Revelation 12:11). Notice the past tense – they 'overcame' the
devil by the blood of the Lamb and by the word of their testimony.
Every believer has already overcome the devil, by virtue of the
blood that speaks better things. The word of our testimony is not
so much our story as our testimony of the holy blood. The Holy
Spirit bears witness to the blood, and we are to bear witness to the
blood: by doing so we enforce Christ's victory over the devil.

We do not fight for victory. We stand in Christ's victory, forc-
ing the demonic realm to do what they are legally bound to do:
that is, to obey. The outworking of the cross means those who
embrace the cross of Christ are no longer captives to the devil but
are free to serve the living God.

Our testimony is like hyssop.

*Hyssop. A species of marjoram and a member of the mint family.
Hyssop was an aromatic shrub under one metre (three feet) tall with
clusters of yellow flowers. It grew in rocky crevices and was cultivated
on terraced walls (1 Kings 4:33). Bunches of hyssop were used to*

sprinkle blood on the doorposts in Egypt (Exodus 12:22), and in purification ceremonies (Leviticus 14:4, 6, 51–2). David mentioned it as an instrument of inner cleansing (Psalm 51:7). It was used at the crucifixion to relieve Jesus' thirst (John 19:29). The hyssop was very similar to the caper plant. It is sometimes rendered marjoram by the NEB.

(*Nelson's Illustrated Bible Dictionary*, Thomas Nelson Publishers, 1986)

The children of Israel were told that God was going to kill all the firstborn in Egypt; after that, Pharaoh would release them from slavery in Egypt. So that they would be protected, they were instructed to take bunches of hyssop and use it to splash the blood of a lamb on their doorposts and lintels. The angel of death saw the blood and passed over that house. Use your testimony of the blood of Christ to protect you, your property and your health.

I find it helpful to confess out loud these facts:

- I testify that the blood of Christ has forgiven all my sins.
- I testify that by His wounds (blood) I am healed.
- I testify that every curse is broken, that my family and I are free because Christ has delivered us by His own blood from the curse of the law (Deuteronomy 28): 'Christ redeemed us from the curse of the law by becoming a curse for us, for it is written: "Cursed is everyone who is hung on a tree" ' (Galatians 3:13).
- I testify that Christ's blood has given me access to the very throne-room of God.
- I testify that I have already overcome the devil by Christ's holy blood.
- I apply that blood to my house. Thank you, Lord, that the devil must pass over us and cannot enter into this property.

There have been many people who have 'applied the blood' in this way and seen it work. It will work for you, too.

I want to end this chapter on the Warrior's Winning Ways with nine steps to freedom, and with Colin Urquhart's 'prayer and faith declaration' from his book *The Truth That Sets You Free* (Hodder & Stoughton, 1993). You will notice that many of the steps to freedom are the antidotes to the ways I have mentioned in which the devil seeks to oppress Christians.

Nine Steps to Freedom

- *Truth* Then you will know the truth, and the truth will set you free' (John 8:32). We need to know and believe the truth of God's Word. 'And God raised us up with Christ and seated us with him in the heavenly realms in Christ Jesus' (Ephesians 2:6).
- *Repentance* 'If we confess our sins, he is faithful and just and will forgive us our sins and purify us from all unrighteousness' (1 John 1:9). Take this seriously. The devil is a legalist. Confess and receive God's forgiveness. 'As far as the east is from the west, so far has he removed our transgressions from us' (Psalm 103:12).
- *Forgiving heart* 'And when you stand praying, if you hold any-thing against anyone, forgive him, so that your Father in heaven may forgive you your sins' (Mark 11:25). One songwriter wrote: 'Forgive or forget it!' We need to speak out our forgiveness. The decision needs to be made regardless of feelings. God will back up our decision with action. 'Do not take revenge, my friends, but leave room for God's wrath, for it is written: "It is mine to avenge; I will repay," says the Lord' (Romans 12:19). 'Bless those who persecute you; bless and do not curse' (Romans 12:14).
- *Renounce Satan and his works* Pray and bind yourself to Jesus. Speak it out loud: 'I renounce you, Satan. I have nothing more

to do with you or your works of darkness. I bind myself to Jesus for ever.'

- *Walk in the truth*   Make a covenant with the Lord that you will obey everything you understand from the Word of God. 'He said to them, "Go into all the world and preach the good news to all creation"' (Mark 16:15). Start to do it. 'Do not be anxious about anything, but in everything, by prayer and petition, with thanksgiving, present your requests to God' (Philippians 4:6). No more worry; enter into freedom.
- *Stay in a 'live' church*   Be rooted and serve your brothers and sisters in that place.
- *Honour your father and mother*   Do all you can to honour them. Thank God that He has chosen your parents for you.
- *Resist Satan*   'Submit yourselves, then, to God. Resist the devil, and he will flee from you' (James 4:7).
- *Daily confession*   Confess daily the truth of God's Word over your life and family.

Prayer and Faith Declaration

In the Name of Jesus and through the victory of the cross I stand against any habitual sin in my life and the bondage that has resulted from this.

Heavenly Father, I repent of this sin (name it …). I choose to turn away from it so that my life may no longer be under its influence, and that I shall no longer grieve you in this way. Please forgive me for any way in which this sin has given the devil opportunity in my life, and for the ways in which my sins have influenced others negatively.

I choose to submit my heart afresh to you that you might work change in my life.

Thank you, Father, that I am yoked together with Jesus. I want to be more like Him. Change me into His likeness from one degree of glory to another.

In the name of Jesus and by the power of His blood I come against every enemy stronghold in my thinking. I have the mind of Christ, and choose to submit my thinking to the Truth of God's Word.

In particular I come against the stronghold of (name them …). I now use the spiritual weapons that are mighty to the pulling down of strongholds and everything in my life which sets itself up against the knowledge of Christ. I believe those strongholds are now pulled down. I choose to submit my mind to the truth of God's Word. I will not allow any fresh strongholds of unbelief or negativity to be established in my thinking, with your grace and help.

In the name of Jesus and by the power of His blood I now exercise the authority given me by Jesus Christ, and I break the power of any and every curse brought against me, or any member of the family to which I belong. The power of that curse is broken, and I and the members of my family are delivered completely from any influences this has had on our lives.

I choose to bless all who have sought to curse me.

I praise you, Heavenly Father, that I do not need to live in any fear of the devil or future curse. You are my shield and I praise you for the victory you give me over every device of the evil one through Jesus.

9 The Warrior's Stand

Stand over Millions

A Baptist millionaire businessman received a prophesy from a visiting preacher that the devil was about to attack his finances and that he would need to stand his ground against this demonic onslaught. (God will warn us if we are open to listen.) Overnight, the head chef walked out of one of his most prestigious restaurants. Others followed, profits dipped, then the stock market began to fall.

To 'stand' is mentioned three times in Ephesians 6. How long should you stand? For as long as it takes. This man stood and confessed the Lordship of Jesus over his businesses for a full two years, when the same preacher brought a word from God to him that the attack was over and the victory was assured. Within days that word came to pass; everything was returned to normal.

This man uses his money for the spread of the gospel, and the enemy tried to stop him doing this. He stood as a warrior and saw the victory. Many would have given up, possibly claiming it was God's will to keep them poor so that they could learn humility. But this man knew that what he was facing was a demonic attack. When you face a demonic attack – and we will all do so at some time – be a warrior and don't run away. Stand and fight with faith and a good confession, and you too will be victorious.

I was feeling wretched, burnt out, vulnerable. Then God gave me a vision, an impression, He showed me that I was clothed in armour. It was an incredible experience.

Stand in Your Armour

When a knight rides out in shining armour on a big white steed to rescue the maiden, no one actually knows what size he is. No one can see him because his armour covers him completely. When the devil sees you, what does he see? He sees the armour. Our lives are hidden with Christ in God. That armour is a description of the Lord Jesus Christ Himself. When I appreciated this, I was greatly encouraged because I realized that even though I was feeling unwell I was still a protected person.

'Therefore put on the full armour of God, so that when the day of evil comes, you may be able to stand your ground, and after you have done everything, to stand' (Ephesians 6:13). Without the armour we will not be able to stand, but with the protective, offensive armour we can begin to stand our ground. Our war is against unseen spirits, and we wrestle them for ourselves and for others.

Wrestling was a popular sport in the days when Paul was writing, and there are many things in the nature of wrestling which are true of the battle and warfare we are involved in today. The struggle continues until somebody is pinned to the mat; fitness is of the utmost importance. A lot of it is put on, but much of it is real. Professional wrestlers get cauliflower ears, broken bones and all kinds of injuries – it is a demanding contact sport. We are wrestling against evil spirits and we need to have a long-term determination and commitment. You cannot wrestle successfully in fits and starts!

When we are in a tough situation it is easy to escape into a daydream land, avoiding reality by going into fantasy. That is running away. When confronted with demonic problems, you must stand and face them. We have to stand our ground against anything that comes against us: against temptations, past sinful patterns and failures. We will not enter into Christ's victory until we stand.

Stand Shielded

Above all else, take up the shield of faith. God has surrounded us with a shield of favour. God is a shield for His people. Do you know that, as you sit and read this book, you have a shield of protection? Thoughts can come to you from God or from the devil. We can be tricked by the devil, because the devil tries to imitate and impress us to the point that we think it is easier to hear what he is saying that to hear the Lord. That has to be the biggest lie he has ever told. God loves to communicate to us and speak to us. That is why He has given us His Word, the Bible.

Jesus said we have got to be like children – not childish, but like children – and those who trust God like children are the ones who hear God's voice more often and more clearly. Right from day one, I was bold enough to believe that God wanted to speak to me, but some people get so complicated about it. Keep simple about the whole issue of God speaking. He speaks in diverse ways and He speaks to different people in different ways, but He will communicate with us. Some people tell me the devil has been chasing them all week. They are able to relate to me for hours what the devil has been telling them, but the same people will often say, 'I can't hear God's voice, He doesn't speak to me.'

As we become like children, we become intimate with the Lord. I asked one person what God had done for him that day, and he replied, 'He smiled and waved to me.' I love that – it is so intimate. God speaks to us more clearly than the devil. God is speaking to us all the time, encouraging, affirming and correcting us. If we exercise faith for healing, finances and forgiveness of sins, we can exercise faith to hear God's voice. It is not a question of striving and getting into a struggle; the more tense you get, the less you will hear. It is a question of tuning in and listening. God is talking all the time. 'Call to me and I will answer you and tell you great and unsearchable things you do not know' (Jeremiah 33:3). 'Without faith it is impossible to please God' (Hebrews 11:6).

Stand against Fear and Imaginations

I stood my ground against fear. After six months of standing, the fear was beaten. Stand your ground against the fear of man. If anybody tries to manipulate or control you, say no. Stand your ground!. If we allow people to control us, they will. If we want to enter into the plans and purposes of God, we have to let our 'yes' be 'yes' and our 'no' be 'no'. If we say yes when we mean no because we are frightened of people or we don't want to offend or hurt them, we will be nicer than God. If we are always trying not to offend people, we won't fulfil our mission in life, we will not be free. That does not mean that we have to be rude to people, but it does means that our 'yes' is 'yes' and our 'no' is 'no'.

There is a new breed coming in the earth. Not wimps, but warriors. Although we live in the world, we do not wage war as the world does. 'The weapons we fight with are not the weapons of the world. On the contrary, they have divine power to demolish strongholds. We demolish arguments and every pretension that sets itself up against the knowledge of God, and we take captive every thought to make it obedient to Christ' (2 Corinthians 10:4–5). When an argument is going on in our minds, we can demolish it.

A group of teenagers were being taught at a YWAM training session. The teacher said, 'Come on! Cast those imaginations down.' I thought, if they can do it, then I can do it. It is a question of being in control of your own mind. We can bring our minds in subjection to Jesus Christ by using our God-given authority. We take captive every thought and make it obedient to Christ, and we will be ready to punish every act of disobedience once our obedience is complete.

You have to deal in prayer with the pretensions in other people's lives before they will listen to you about the gospel. I have experienced people who, as I speak to them, are telling me proud and vain imaginations. So I begin to pray and cast down those pretentious thoughts, not loudly but in my mind and praying that I will get an opportunity to speak to them about Jesus. Once our obedience is complete we can bring people into an obedience to Christ. That is the way it works. Whatever you have got, you can give. There is a way made for the Word of God to penetrate their hearts, and then they have to choose for themselves.

Stand against Strongholds

Usually it is a stronghold built up in the mind from the past. It can be cast down, defeated and destroyed by the truth. I used to think people were talking about me. I would often go and ask them; 95 per cent of the time they would say no, and the spiritual warfare going on in my mind would be diffused by truth. If I am thinking a critical thought about somebody, I can't go up to them and say, 'I have a critical thought about you!' If I am thinking some weird stuff I can take authority in prayer against those thoughts, and I don't have to tell you what is going on in my mind. We do not know what goes on in the mind of another: that is God's order, God's blessing.

Share any strongholds in your mind with someone you trust. You don't have to share all the details, just share the problem. Then say, 'Let's pray together and let's dethrone these thoughts until they are no more. We bring these strongholds into submission to Christ.'

There are some vital positions that you must never give up, where you must never give ground. One of the main line of attack is the mind. We have to pray, aggressively pulling down imaginations that do not agree with the Word of God. Speak to these spurious arguments 'in the Name of Jesus'. 'We demolish arguments and every pretension that sets itself up against the knowledge of God, and we take captive every thought to make it obedient to Christ' (2 Corinthians 10:5) – our mind, thoughts and imaginations. 'Take the helmet of salvation' (Ephesians 6:17).

Stand Your Ground

Some people are privileged to attend church where the Spirit of God is moving; they are thoroughly blessed. However, instead of staying rooted in that place for any length of time, they go from church to church, never settling. Every church will go through cleansing, purging and character development, and during hard times some people begin to leave the church. They say, 'This wasn't what I expected.' So they change church. Of course, sometimes we are meant to leave, but if we move on when things get tough something is wrong. People who do not work things through do not grow much.

Those who stand their ground and stick with the church and partner where God has placed them will grow. To mature, we have to move, from consumerism, from receiving alone, to a lifestyle of giving. Hardship and sacrifice enable us to develop character. We move from babyhood into parenting. As the saying goes, 'When the going gets tough, the tough get going!' The devil is always seeking to fire his flaming missiles at us, and I have listed some of the more common ones against which we have to stand.

- Stand your ground against offences, resentments.
- Stand your ground against jealousy.
- Stand your ground against confusion.
- Stand your ground against fear.
- Stand your ground against accusation and condemnation.
- Stand your ground against sickness.
- Stand your ground against poverty.
- Stand your ground against failure.

Many people are caught in the 'putting out fires' syndrome: they wait for a crisis to occur before taking action. Do something to offset the crisis before it happens, and it will not happen.

Jesus said, pray to be delivered from temptation before the temptation happens, before the devil's schemes come upon you, before you get into a crisis. How many of you know that it is not good to live in crisis all the time? When you pray, you can even know what the schemes of the devil are, and before they are even hatched out you have already dealt with them.

In our former church, our senior pastor taught the church to pray for an hour in tongues for the saints; he called this 'pastoral prayer'. When this happened, the church problems would be radically reduced during the following week. Paul called it 'praying in the Spirit'. We are demolishing the devil's strongholds. We are destroying his schemes and plans against us. When we spend time praying in the Spirit, we find the devil's plans are often thwarted before they ever get started.

Stand with God's Plan and Purpose

The Lord has a plan for us, but so does the devil. 'Let no one be found among you who sacrifices his son or daughter in the fire, who practices divination or sorcery, interprets omens, engages in witchcraft, or casts spells, or who is a medium or spiritist or who consults the dead. Anyone who does these things is detestable to the LORD' (Deuteronomy 18:10–12). God forbids it because they are part of the devil's plan. Such plans are always destructive, although he may put a carrot in front of us and offer us the kingdoms of the world.

No divination is allowed: if we delve into any form of divination we will open ourselves to the devil's plan. I was deeply involved in the occult. It is like a spider's web, a web of intrigue. You put one finger in and you are caught. Many go deeper and deeper until, in the end, the spider consumes them. The only way of escape is to come to Christ. There is a way out, but only through repentance, renouncing and forsaking of all occult practices. If you have been involved and have turned to Christ, destroy or burn all occult literature and trappings. Receive prayer from a minister of the gospel to break and dismiss all dark spirits.

God is a good God and He has a good plan. Sometimes it can be a bit tough on the flesh! It is a bit tough when the devil is opposing us, but at the end God's plan is really fulfilling and exciting. I really enjoy what I do, although I admit I do not enjoy fighting the devil every day and putting the flesh down, especially when I have to deal with pride and humble myself. What I do enjoy is the exciting adventure of doing God's will. After I've witnessed to somebody or I've served the Lord, I feel a rush. I sense that I have fulfilled my destiny for that day.

I was involved in all kinds of exciting things in the world, but they all turned sour on me. They were like a mirage: I went for them and they were not what they appeared to be. With the Lord, there is no disappointment, only a reality. We are warned, 'Do not give the devil a foothold' (Ephesians 4:27). The devil wants us to walk in his ways, and so the Bible tells us not to give him a place.

Stand against Offences

If you look at various scriptures they speak about the devil's schemes. The devil has plans and schemes to trap Christians. He has laid snares and traps. The Bible speaks about the word 'offence'. 'Then He said to the disciples, "It is impossible that no offences should come, but woe to him through whom they do come!"' (Luke 17:1, NKJ). 'An offence' in Greek is *scandalon*, which is like a tasty morsel of meat that is set before us. It looks good, but when you reach out to take it you become entrapped.

The devil has traps set up for each one of us. Supposing even now somebody is offending you. You have got two choices. The devil has set up that offence to trap you, and if you get angry, you will fall into that pit. It is part of the warfare that we are wise enough to know what to do when an offence comes. You may be tempted to resent the offence, to rise up and get angry. Or you may meditate on the hurt and the thing that has been done against you. That gives birth to bitterness and hatred, and down into the pit you go. There is only one way out of that pit. Our brothers and sisters can reach down into the pit and try to get us out, but there is only one power on earth who can get us out from there. That is the blood of Jesus: repentance and faith will bring us up out of the pit.

Has anyone tried to wind you up recently? The devil is always seeking to wind us up. That is his aim. He knows that if he winds us up he's got us; he has us pinned by the shoulders to the ground, as happens in wrestling. Take the second choice: stand your ground, refuse the temptation to resent the offender. Flow in the fruit of love, forgive. Then take authority over the spirits behind the offence. When Peter attempted to stop Jesus going to the cross, Jesus said, 'You are an offence to me,' and then rebuked Satan. He knew it was a spiritual power behind Peter's action and took authority to dismiss its influence.

Stand against Temptation

I like the story of the holy man who had a banana. He was walking along to the river to bathe, and on the way he met a monkey. He said to the monkey, 'Hold this banana, and if you can hold it but not eat it until I come back then you will be holy.'

The monkey thought to himself, 'This is easy. All I have to do is hold and not eat the banana, and I can then be holy.'

The holy man went on his way to bathe and the monkey stayed behind, looking at the banana. 'What did the holy man say? I must not eat the banana. Well, he did not say I shouldn't look at it. What a lovely banana. And he didn't say I shouldn't stroke the banana.' The monkey began to stroke the juicy banana. 'I mustn't eat the banana but I can smell it. I want to look at you, you're so beautiful. What a lovely smell. He didn't say I shouldn't open, smell or look at it.'

The monkey's digestive juices began to flow, and the smell and taste of the banana were just too much for our poor friend. When the holy man returned, there was not a trace of the banana left.

This is the way that temptation works. We are told not to do certain things; Adam and Eve were told not to eat the fruit of the tree of life. When the devil came to Eve he said, 'Look!' She looked and began to meditate on the fruit. The devil gets us to meditate on that which he wants to get us to get involved with. We think we can play with certain things and we will be all right. It is a progressive thing – you do not backslide in one day, it is a process. The devil begins to put things before our eyes. He may put the same resentful thought about a person before you for months before you fall into the pit. Therefore we have to be aware of his devices and not meditate upon the things that he brings to our attention. This is why it is so important to meditate on the right things. 'Finally, brothers, whatever is true, whatever is noble, whatever is right, whatever is pure, whatever is lovely, whatever is admirable – if anything is excellent or praiseworthy – think about such things' (Philippians 4:8). If we are to stop thinking negatively about somebody we must start thinking positively, just as the Bible declares: fill your mind with pure, noble thoughts. School yourself and develop a healthy mind.

God sees character. We look at personality and often reject a person because they don't gel with us. There are people we get on with and people we don't. When we don't gel with somebody, we are still to think wholesome thoughts about them. We have got to work at it! If we think the negative, the devil has got us meditating and looking at the banana.

You won't forget this banana story, will you!

Stand Alert, Saint

God wants us to be alert.

> For our struggle is not against flesh and blood, but against the rulers, against the authorities, against the powers of this dark world and against the spiritual forces of evil in the heavenly realms. Therefore put on the full armour of God, so that when the day of evil comes, you may be able to stand your ground, and after you have done everything, to stand. Stand firm then, with the belt of truth.
>
> (Ephesians 6:12–14)

We must be alert and always keep on praying.

'Alert' is a very interesting word. If I had been in Israel when those Scud missiles were coming over from Iraq, I would have been very alert! I would have wanted to see where they landed so that I could run far away. The enemy is firing his Scud missiles all the time. We must be alert and react quickly with our Patriot missiles, putting out the flaming missiles of the enemy. Shoot them down, extinguish those missiles on the shield of faith!

To be alert means to watch intently. Jesus told His followers to 'watch and pray so that you will not fall into temptation' (Mark 14:38). The devil wants us to watch the wrong things, to be taken up with lustful things. God says watch! Watch God, watch our lives, watch the enemy and see where the Scud missiles need to be destroyed. Watching is always with prayer. We should pray all the time. Not that we should be in the prayer room all the time, but that we should be living a prayerful life. If I am about to say or think something negative about someone, I try to catch myself and pray for them instead. If anything negative comes out of my mouth, I question myself: Have I prayed about this? Am I in faith and believing God to do something, or am I being negative and critical?

If you are a pastor you see and hear a lot of problems, but you have to be able to keep yourself free. If you allow the problems to be your meditation, you get burdened. Bring answers and solutions from the Word of God to the people. If you only lock into their problem on a natural level, you are never going to help them, because help only comes from the Lord. However, you can bring a solution by a word from God.

Stand in the Presence of God

Everywhere Jesus went, the presence of God was manifested. Everywhere we go, the presence of God is released. Jesus Christ lives in us and so where we go, He goes, and where He goes, the presence of God is.

Let me teach you the words of a song which express this well:

I'm a blessing everywhere I go.
I'm a blessing everywhere I go.
I'm a blessing everywhere I go.
With Christ in me the world will see
I'm a blessing everywhere I go.

I'm living in the victory.
I'm living in the victory.
I'm living in the victory.
With Christ in me the world will see
I'm living in the victory.

My wife and I were walking down the road when we saw a man approaching us. As he neared us, he let out a piercing scream and ran back the opposite way, still screaming. What happened to him? He walked into the presence of God, and the demons in him began to be tormented.

During our honeymoon on the beautiful island of Penang, we were strolling without a care in the world. Deeply in love, we were not really taking much notice of the things around us. We walked past a beggar, and because he didn't receive anything from us he became angry and began to follow us, cursing us. I didn't understand his language but felt a stirring deep within my spirit.

I felt the indignation of the Holy Spirit. I turned and prayed directly at the beggar, rebuking an evil spirit, and the beggar ran away as fast as his legs could carry him.

The next day he saw us coming, and ran off. Later Joyce told me – that man spoke Joyce's language – that he was cursing us. He said, 'These people are newly married. They are going to die young in a car accident.' I had not known what was being said, but the Spirit of God did, and the man, the demon, the curses were all sent packing at the Name of Jesus.

'When he arrived at the other side in the region of the Gadarenes, two demon-possessed men coming from the tombs met him. They were so violent that no one could pass that way. "What do you want with us, Son of God?" they shouted. "Have you come here to torture us before the appointed time?"' (Matthew 8:28–9). Demons were tormenting the demoniac, but when Jesus came on the scene the situation was reversed. In the presence of God, the demons were the ones being tormented. If you are being tormented by devils, bring them into the presence of God. They will be tormented, and it will not be long before you are free.

A friend from India had been in the mountains, fasting and praying. On his return, he went to buy vegetables at the local market. As he walked through the market the Hindu people began to fall to the ground, manifesting demonic powers. What was happening was not really all that surprising, because something similar is recorded in the Bible at the time of Jesus' arrest.

So Judas came to the grove, guiding a detachment of soldiers and some officials from the chief priests and Pharisees. They were carrying torches, lanterns and weapons.

Jesus, knowing all that was going to happen to him, went out and asked them, 'Who is it you want?'

Jesus of Nazareth,' they replied.

'I am he,' Jesus said. (And Judas the traitor was standing there with them.) When Jesus said, 'I am he,' they drew back and fell to the ground.

(John 18:3–6)

Grown, mature, trained men, soldiers, officers and religious leaders, all fell to the ground. That is the powerful presence of God.

Stand in the Authority of Jesus' Name

In one area of West Malaysia the drug addicts would rob people to support their addictions. A Christian girl was on her way to church when a gang of men tried to grab her handbag. She rebuked the demons in Jesus' Name and all the men fell to the ground. She walked away unharmed, with her handbag still in her possession.

Some churches teach the children to use their authority in Christ. A little girl was abducted by a man. She was dragged into a car, and as the man sped off the girl said to him, 'You must take me back to my mummy, in Jesus' Name.' She repeated this command over and over again. After some time, the man turned the car around, drove back to the spot where he had abducted her, pushed her out of the car and drove off. Christ in us is greater than Satan in the world.

The Indian friend I mentioned earlier was again praying and fasting in the mountains. On the seventeenth day he had a vision of his niece. He saw that she had died, and in his vision he saw her placed on the funeral pyre. His father was desperate to contact his son to tell him what had happened, but this was impossible as he was so far away and there were no communication systems in the mountains. He felt God constraining him to pray that she should be brought back to life, although she had been dead for three days. Nevertheless, while in the mountains the uncle started commanding his niece to come back to life.

The funeral arrangements were going ahead. The grandfather (who was an agnostic) was about to light the pyre when he stopped and amazed the onlookers by saying, 'I call upon the God of my son, Jeevanandan, to bring her back to life.' The little girl opened her eyes, sat up and was restored to her family, alive and well. The grandfather accepted Christ as his Saviour and became a Christian. God's power is still in operation. There is no limit to what He can do.

Stay Standing

My wife and I were in Singapore doing a crusade. During the time of fasting beforehand, we were attacked: we saw demons coming from all over the place to attack us. It was oppressive. As most kids do, I pushed the boundaries.

'This is horrible, Lord,' I grumbled, 'I want to go home.' At the same time the devil was speaking, roaring, 'You're not in the will of God.'

After days of this attitude, the Lord said, 'Okay, go home!' Then I got scared because I knew deep inside that if I were to leave, I really would be out of God's will. But He was allowing me to go. The children of Israel were grumbling and complaining to God about the manna and demanding meat, and it is recorded that God gave them their request 'but sent leanness into their souls' (Psalm 106:15). That is, there was an absence of God's blessing. A lot of Christians demand their own way and do their own thing, but lose the sense of God's presence and God's blessing. After heartfelt repentance, I asked God to let me stay and finish the crusade, and 70 per cent of the pressure that had latched itself to me lifted off when I made that decisive choice. When you choose God's way and stay with it, the same pressure will lift off you.

I can still remember vividly one particular occasion when I messed something up. I was a young Christian and I prophesied in a meeting, and it wasn't from God. The Bible College principal was upset with me, and he summoned me upstairs! I thought, 'I am for it!' I was quaking with fear. At that time I was scared of anyone in authority.

'Lord, You have got to help me!' I cried out desperately. Then I remembered the scripture in Daniel, 'I will shut the lion's mouth.' I went into the principal's office and said, 'I am sorry, I missed it, I was wrong.' I repented.

The principal opened his mouth and was going to tear into me, but he did not say anything. I was amazed. God had truly 'shut the lion's mouth'.

Stand until Mature

God wants us to be mature. When we are mature we will not base our decisions on impulse, because impulsive behaviour gets us into all kinds of destruction. The devil will try to push us to do impulsive things. Instead, we need to do things prayerfully. Sleep on decisions. Think through issues objectively from the Word of God. Take counsel from brothers and sisters.

You have to think through to the point where you know it is the will of God to do and make a particular decision. Once you have made the decision and you know that it is the will of God, you are going to be fruitful. Anything that you do in the will of God is fruitful. I am not saying there won't be trials on the way. There will be! But maturity is saying, 'Devil, you can roar all you like, I don't care what you do. I am not jumping for you or anybody else, and whatever you say and do I am going to stand for the Lord Jesus Christ, come what may!'

10 Living Daily with Angels

Underground Angel

After my father died in 1978 my friend and I decided to go on holiday to St Leonard's, near Hastings. We persuaded my mother into coming with us, as the break would do her good. We were travelling by train and needed to go through London. My mother's next-door neighbours knew London very well. They were going to London the same Saturday. We all went together, using the Underground to get across London to our designated station.

The way to the Underground was down a very steep escalator. We all had our cases on luggage trolleys. We got separated, with thousands of people clambering around the station. My mum was the first to land at the bottom of the escalator, but she didn't get off. She had pulled the trolley off the moving staircase, but it pulled her backwards and she landed on her back. She was unable to get off the moving floor as her raincoat had become caught and was being sucked into the escalator. In an instant, a tall man appeared behind my mother, untangled her raincoat, picked her up off the escalator with her luggage, all in one go, and put her in a safe place near the wall. We saw it all happen as we came down the escalator. The man was dressed in a long trench-coat which touched the floor and a trilby-type hat, pulled down over his face. He didn't speak a word.

He disappeared as my mother was about to thank him very much. The man seemed to arrive from nowhere – he hadn't passed us on the escalator – but when he was needed he was there! If my mother had been lying helpless on the bottom of the escalator for much longer, her neck could easily have been broken. As it was, all she had was a slightly sore neck and a very chewed-up new raincoat. Only afterwards did we realize who the 'man' in the trench-coat was. He was an angel.

Mrs A. Perry

Angel of the Lord

'The angel of the LORD encamps around those who fear him, and he delivers them' (Psalm 34:7). The mighty angels are sent by God to enable us to fulfil God's will. When we meet the condition we can claim the promise of angelic encampments with total deliverance. That means angels will make their camp with us, live with us day and night. Their very presence will guarantee our safety and will be enough to deliver us from all evil.

Approximately five years ago my husband and I were travelling from the south coast to the Midlands at the end of the summer holiday. Before we set off we committed our journey to the Lord, asking for His angelic protection and that He would give His angels charge over us. We had our four children aged between five and sixteen with us in our small car and the roof rack was loaded with our luggage.

As we travelled along the busy M23 in the fast lane, a suitcase suddenly toppled from the roof rack, landing behind us in the road. It was immediately hit by a car. Another car also hit the case, strewing the contents along the centre lane. We were able to get over to the hard shoulder.

The holiday traffic thundered past and I told the children it was far too dangerous for them to try and retrieve their belongings. Our daughter was becoming distressed as she saw her possessions being destroyed by the traffic.

I sat in the back of the car with our five-year-old son and cried to God for His help. Within seconds a van pulled up on the hard shoulder and a man with a fluorescent jacket got out. He walked into the middle lane and stood and faced the traffic with his arms outstretched. A juggernaut juddered to a halt and the traffic on the centre and inside lanes stopped. My husband and children ran backwards and forwards, collecting our daughter's belongings. We were cramming them into the boot of the car when the man drove past us and disappeared with the traffic. We had no conversation with him and were unable to thank him.

As we drove the rest of the journey we pondered over what had happened and realized we had been helped by an angel. No person would attempt to stop the traffic on the motorway by walking into the centre lane with his hand up, yet the whole scene had looked completely natural. As the traffic had come to a stop there had been no collision and no cars had changed lanes. We realized afresh that these helpers and protectors God has given can look like ordinary people, but even their supernatural powers look natural!

Anon

Do you require an angel to deliver you? You may reply, 'Yes!' right away, but we need to meet the conditions and be those who fear God. This gives us an insight into why some are so utterly blessed and others continually struggle. But first, let us look at what the fear of God is not.

No Fear in Love

In this way, love is made complete among us so that we will have confidence on the day of judgement, because in this world we are like him. There is no fear in love. But perfect love drives out fear, because fear has to do with punishment. The one who fears is not made perfect in love. We love because he first loved us.

(1 John 4:17–19)

God is love. Those who know God's love have no fear of punishment. Confidence in God's love equips us with boldness even in the day of judgement. If we are confident before God, we will be equally confident before people. God once asked me if I was afraid of Him. 'No!' was my swift response. Then why was I sometimes afraid of those who have lesser rank or position than He has? God has it all, all wisdom, power and holiness. It dawned on me that, because I am not afraid of God, I need not fear anyone. The fear of the Lord is not the fear of punishment or judgement.

'For God has not given us a spirit of fear, but of power and of love and of a sound mind' (2 Timothy 1:7, NKJ). There is a spirit of fear. Possibly 70–80 per cent of the world's population has been plagued with this spirit and has known abnormal fears at some time. A healthy fear occurs when danger threatens – it may well save your life – but an evil spirit produces an unhealthy fear, not for action but for inertia. Possibly 90 per cent of fear-based images never materialize: they do not happen. Many people live in constant torment. The fear of death, the fear of failure, the fear of authorities – we could compile pages of different fears, but all are rooted in a two-fold satanic scheme. First, to convince Christians that God does not love them. Confidence is lost and the door opened to a fear of punishment. Second, he seeks to deceive us into believing his fears.

Saved from Wrath

'Since we have now been justified by his blood, how much more shall we be saved from God's wrath through him!' (Romans 5:9). Since we shall be saved from wrath through Him (through His life) we are totally justified *just as if we had never sinned* and released for ever from God's anger. God is angry with sinners, but those of us who have received Jesus as our personal Saviour have been delivered from this righteous anger. Jesus became our sin offering, and God's righteous anger against sin was satisfied by what our Saviour did on the cross. It is finished. We are free and do not fear punishment any longer.

The way to defeat the second strategy of the enemy when he tries to deceive us into believing his fears is: 'In addition to all this, take up the shield of faith, with which you can extinguish all the flaming arrows of the evil one' (Ephesians 6:16). When fear knocks on the door, answer it with faith. 'Submit yourselves, then, to God. Resist the devil, and he will flee from you' (James 4:7). Rebuke, resist this wicked spirit. Recognize your enemy and pray aggressively against him. Cast him out.

Fear of Authorities

I was travelling at 30 miles an hour in a built-up area, glanced in my rear mirror and saw a police car following me. I panicked and fear gripped me – but why was I afraid? After all, I was keeping the right speed limit. Before Christ (BC) I had been in trouble with the police on occasions, and I have been on the wrong side of threats and rough treatment, I realized that I was being abnormally scared and I took this to the Lord in prayer. We must face fear with faith, and for the next five to six months I rebuked, resisted and confronted this paralysing fear.

One morning at church, two burly policemen burst into the outside foyer. 'Where's the fire?' they demanded. But there was no fire, it was a hoax call.

After dealing with the two policemen for about 20 minutes, I realized there was not a trace of fear. I no longer fear the police, praise God! Since then other fears have been discarded by the same prayer truths. You can learn to change a thought, image or picture of fear. Some may see themselves in a car accident, and this is a nagging fear for them. If this or something similar is your problem, tell yourself: I am not dying now. See yourself laughing, running and very much alive.

The Word of God

Another effective weapon against the wrong kind of fear is the Word of God. What demonic negative can survive with Psalm 91? Write it out, read it aloud, believe it as it is written. 'I will say of the LORD, "He is my refuge and fortress, my God in whom I trust." ' The Word of God is razor sharp and deadly accurate! Use it to stop the spirit of fear.

'Applying your heart to understanding' (Proverbs 2:2). Application of God's word is often lacking. There are lots of sermons, books, tapes, but not so many who apply God's Word to their daily living.

'Therefore everyone who hears these words of mine and puts them into practice is like a wise man who built his house on the rock' (Matthew 7:24). Take courage if you are laying these good, deep foundations: you may experience cost now, but when a crisis comes, you and your family or even your ministry will stand and remain unshaken. Not so for the foolish, compromising, superficial Christian – his foundation is built on movable sand. In the crisis of life (they come to all of us sooner or later!) the foundation will move and that believer will become another casualty, and this happens all too often. People backslide, die prematurely, marriages fail, relationships are in turmoil. This does not explain why these things happen to all believers, but it does give understanding for the many who have no true foundation. We cannot follow the Lord on our terms, do whatever we want with our lives, and still squeeze into heaven.

Hear and Understand the Truth

'Listen then to what the parable of the sower means: When anyone hears the message about the kingdom and does not understand it, the evil one comes and snatches away what was sown in his heart. This is the seed sown along the path' (Matthew 13:18–19). The sower is said to sow the Word of God. Jesus said that if we understand this story then we will understand all the other parables. This, then, is the prince of all parables, worthy of our time and avid attention. 'To the Jews who had believed him, Jesus said, "If you hold to my teaching, you are really my disciples. Then you will know the truth, and the truth will set you free"' (John 8:31–2). It is not the truth that makes us and keeps us free, but the knowing (understanding) of truth. How many times did you hear the Word of God regarding salvation before understanding it, acting on it and receiving genuine salvation?

The truth may have been proclaimed but not yet understood. 'When anyone hears the message about the kingdom and does not understand it, the evil one comes and snatches away what was sown in his heart' (Matthew 13:19).

'But the one who received the seed that fell on good soil is the man who hears the word and understands it. He produces a crop, yielding a hundred, sixty or thirty times what was sown' (Matthew 13:23). That is increase. Do we want to be fruitful? Apply your heart to understanding, and your will. Even if the answer is delayed, it will come to pass. God's delays are not God's denials!

The Fear of the Lord

So far we have been looking at the wrong types of fear and how to deal with it, but what is the fear of the Lord which enables angels to build camps around us and our homes?

It is an awe, a heartfelt, respectful, reverence of our God. This is sadly lacking in many modern Christian circles today. A attractive young university student opened her heart to me, and the problem she shared was soon solved through God's words. However, during our time together I questioned her about her morality at the university. 'I never sleep around,' she stated adamantly. 'I love and respect my father too much to bring shame to his name.' She was talking about her own earthly father, but a light went on in my mind. This was the parallel to the reverential respect we should have towards our heavenly Father. Out of respect and love we do not sin, not wanting to bring shame to His name. The adultery of David is still flaunted in the cinema thousands of years later! Every action has a knock-on effect, for God or for the enemy. Our church, our families and the nation are depending on us to stand, to hallow and respect our heavenly Father (Matthew 6) and stay free from shameful ways.

Our approach to God is to be full of confidence, boldness and awe. He is the Lord and we are the saved ones. Both the friendship of God and the authority of God are displayed to us, his own children. What He tells us to do, we obey. He is the most exciting God in the universe, the most adventurous, hilarious, holy-wise, loving God, but if we want the angel of the Lord's presence to deliver us, we are to respect and fear Him.

'The fear of the Lord is the beginning of wisdom' (Proverbs 9:10). There are so many benefits to the fear of the Lord that it surprises me that Christians do not hunger and thirst for it! 'Fear the LORD, you his saints, for those who fear him lack nothing. Come, my children, listen to me; I will teach you the fear of the LORD' (Psalm 34:9, 11). God is willing to teach us but are we willing to learn the fear of the Lord?

In Kenya, the students will bow their heads when they present their work to the teacher, as a sign of respect. The bow is making a statement: you are the teacher and I am the student. When some Christians approach God, they will act as if they are the teacher. No, we are the students, we have come to learn. God says, 'Come, listen.' We are not to do all the speaking, and certainly not to delude ourselves that we know it all. We know so little, even those who know the most; there is always so much more to know about God. If we ask Him, God will teach us the fear of the Lord. In asking, come to God and be willing to listen. We will start a tremendous adventure in learning directly from God.

But how do we know if the fear of the Lord is in our lives? I have listed a few check points.

- 'To fear the LORD is to hate evil' (Proverbs 8:13).
- 'He whose walk is upright fears the LORD' (Proverbs 14:2).
- 'Fear of man will prove to be a snare, but whoever trusts in the LORD is kept safe' (Proverbs 29:25).
- 'My son, if you accept my words and store up my commands within you, turning your ear to wisdom and applying your heart to understanding, and if you call out for insight and cry aloud for understanding, and if you look for it as for silver and search for it as for hidden treasure, then you will understand the fear of the LORD and find the knowledge of God' (Proverbs 2:1–5).

To summarize: do you hate sin, do you hate evil? Is your walk an upright one? Do you accept God's words and store them in your heart? Are you calling out to God for wisdom, insight and understanding? Will you apply and live by God's Word on a daily basis? Then you will know the fear of the Lord, with all of its benefits.

Receive All God Has for You

Many Christians receive part of God's Word, but stop short of receiving all that God has for them. The fear of the Lord is certainly not a popular subject nowadays, but it is vital. Imagine you are attending a conference and the following seminars are announced. Which one would you choose to go to?

1   Love, courtship and marriage
2   Healing
3   How to walk in love
4   How to succeed in business
5   The fear of the Lord
6   How to be holy

How many believers would choose to go to seminars 5 and 6? Many would choose the others. (It has happened at seminars!) There are so many benefits to walking in the fear of the Lord and following a lifestyle of holiness. Solomon asked God for wisdom to govern the people of God. God said, 'Because you have asked for wisdom and not riches or honour, I will give you wisdom with riches and honour.' If we receive God's words about the fear of the Lord, it could be that we may not need healing – ever!

'My son, if you receive my words, and treasure my commands within you' (Proverbs 2:2, NKJ). What we treasure is an indication of our heart condition. Four people dug through the roof of Mary's house: 'Since they could not get him to Jesus because of the crowd, they made an opening in the roof above Jesus and, after digging through it, lowered the mat the paralysed man was lying on. When Jesus saw their faith, he said to the paralytic, 'Son, your sins are forgiven' (Mark 2:4–5). Jesus didn't rebuke them, nor did He ask them for money to repair the roof. He saw their faith and healed the paralysed man. That showed where His heart was. The kingdom of God was first place, not the roof. Someone had to repair it later. Do we treasure His words within us, 'turning our ear to wisdom' (Proverbs 2:2)? God's words are a treasure when kept in the heart, meditated and acted on, and they are the source of true wisdom.

'If any of you lacks wisdom, he should ask God, who gives generously to all without finding fault, and it will be given to him' (James 1:5). God's wisdom is first of all pure, and will keep us sanctified. It is so important, what we allow into our hearts, what we see and hear. If we allow rubbish to come in, rubbish will come out. If we treasure God's Word in our heart, out will come wise counsel and wise conduct.

'If you look for it [discernment and understanding] as for silver and search for it as for hidden treasure' (Proverbs 2:4). Gerald Coates once quoted Malcolm Muggeridge, 'You charismatics, you think you know all about God, you take the mystery out of it!' There is always going to be a mystery about God, because God is beyond reason and far beyond finite mankind. We are deluding ourselves with pride if we think that we know it all. We will never, never know it all. We are mere men, and God is God. We need to seek, to seek and seek again after the treasures of knowing God. Only those who hunger and thirst for Him will truly know His character. Is your Christian life boring? Then stir yourself up to seek God, to knock and to search after Him again.

God's Rewards

God 'rewards those who earnestly seek him' (Hebrews 11:6). Earnestly and persistently seek Him. Seeking, searching, humility, hungering, thirsting, will be rewarded at last. 'Then you will understand the fear of the LORD and find the knowledge of God'

(Proverbs 2:5). What a quest! To be a passionate, wise disciple of our Master, Jesus.

The fear of the Lord has multiple benefits. If you live in the fear of God, it will keep you from deception, racism, injustice, a wrong use of your time and tongue. It will guard your life. Are you a seeker of these treasures?

- 'The fear of the LORD is the beginning of wisdom' (Proverbs 9: 10). You will be known for wisdom. The fear of the Lord is clean.
- 'The fear of the LORD is the beginning of knowledge' (Proverbs 1:7).
- 'Do not be wise in your own eyes; fear the Lord and shun evil. This will bring health to your body and nourishment to your bones' (Proverbs 3:7–8). Here's healing!
- 'The fear of the LORD adds length to life' (Proverbs 10:27). We can live longer – that's God's blessing.
- 'He whose walk is upright fears the LORD' (Proverbs 14:2). Walk in uprightness, right-standing with God and mankind.
- 'The fear of the LORD is a fountain of life, turning a man from the snares of death' (Proverbs 14:27).
- 'A wise man's heart guides his mouth, and his lips promote instruction' (Proverbs 16:23).
- 'Humility and the fear of the LORD bring wealth and honour and life' (Proverbs 22:4).
- 'The LORD delights in those who fear him' (Psalm 147:11). You can please the Almighty – what a privilege!
- 'Since they hated knowledge and did not choose to fear the Lord' (Proverbs 1:29). The fear of God is a choice, a heart issue we daily choose, to reverence, respect and obey. If we refuse, he will eventually refuse us.

- 'But since you rejected me when I called and no one gave heed when I stretched out my hand' (Proverbs 1:24). God's heart is one hundred per cent for us. He is faithful and loyal to us. He expects us to listen to Him to be wise.
- Wrong choices always produce consequences, God is not to be trifled or toyed with. He is God and will always have the last word.

> Since you ignored all my advice and would not accept my rebuke, I in turn will laugh at your disaster; I will mock when calamity overtakes you – when calamity overtakes you like a storm, when disaster sweeps over you like a whirlwind, when distress and trouble overwhelm you. Then they will call to me but I will not answer; they will look for me but will not find me. Since they hated knowledge and did not choose to fear the LORD, since they would not accept my advice and spurned my rebuke, they will eat the fruit of their ways and be filled with the fruit of their schemes. For the waywardness of the simple will kill them, and the complacency of fools will destroy them.
>
> (Proverbs 1:25–32)

Come and listen to God and learn the fear of the Lord. We make decisions every day, so let us choose the fear of God today. Enter in, with or without feelings, with or without finesse or understanding. It is not how you begin but how you finish that counts. Start as you are, then God will take you where you could never go without Him. Enjoy angelic encampments all around you and be a protected person. The benefits of the fear of God will be your witness to a godless, dying world, and you will be a fragrance to all, a true aroma of God's life and vitality. You will live daily with a godly protective hedge and shield, and have His holy angels surrounding you and your family day and night.

11 Angels and the Great Harvest

My Wife's Uncle's Witness

My wife's uncle was living and studying in India, where, under the caste system, poor people are not allowed to associate with the rich. He is a Pentecostal believer, a believer in healing and miracles, and he himself was healed of a major incurable disease.

He was called to a situation where a family was in great need. As somebody belonging to the high caste, he was not supposed to go into a low caste area, but he decided to go. He was serving the Lord and there is no class distinction with God. He prayed for one of the family who was very sick. God moved powerfully, and the whole family were showing interest in receiving Jesus.

Suddenly, a large crowd of angry people gathered outside the house and started to shout and throw stones. They declared they were going to enter the house and take and deal with him because he wasn't supposed to be there. He got down on his knees and began to cry out to God for deliverance. The group dispersed, and he was able to lead the whole family to Christ.

Some weeks later one of the neighbours asked him, 'Who was the man standing on the roof that night?'

He replied, 'I don't know what you are talking about.'

The neighbour said, 'The whole crowd saw a huge man standing on the roof. We had wanted to harm you; instead we became scared and ran away. Who was that man?'

'I don't know. I didn't see any man,' he replied. 'I was in the house praying for God to deliver me from the angry mob. Can you describe him?'

The neighbour said: 'He was a good-looking young man, very tall, standing well over six feet, with a mighty appearance of splendour. He was standing with a big drawn sword, and as he looked at us there was fire in his eyes! He also had massive wings at the back and was dressed in white flowing robes. We ran away because we felt the power. We were scared, so we didn't try to harm you.'

Undoubtedly, God sent an angel to deliver Joyce's uncle. In our extremity, when we cry out to God, God is there with the angels. Whether we see them or not, they are there. Joyce's uncle did not see the angel, but the people who were trying to attack him surely did! The same God who healed him of his incurable disease sent an angel to deliver him from an angry mob.

Divine Appointments

God delights to provide us with divine appointments, and angels get involved to help us in preaching the gospel. If we receive and believe God for their intervention, they will be loosed to work on our behalf.

Cornelius was a Roman centurion, a devout man who feared God and prayed to God always.

One day at about three in the afternoon he had a vision. He distinctly saw an angel of God, who came to him and said, 'Cornelius!'

Cornelius stared at him in fear. 'What is it, Lord?' he asked.

The angel answered, 'Your prayers and gifts to the poor have come up as a memorial offering before God. Now send men to Joppa to bring back a man named Simon who is called Peter. He is staying with Simon the tanner, whose house is by the sea.

(Acts 10:3–6)

Why didn't the angel preach the gospel? The angels do not know the grace of salvation so they cannot preach it, but God uses the angels to bring together the ambassadors of the gospel and the sinners who are ready to receive Christ. He was setting up a divine appointment for Peter, and the fruit of this was salvation and baptism of the Holy Spirit.

The whole of Cornelius' family, his household, his servants and friends were all saved the next day. Peter had nothing much to do with it except to be there and share what God had done. God did the rest, and Peter was astounded. Divine appointments leave you like that, amazed and astonished.

Cornelius was a leader with influence, and God wants us to meet leaders of countries and communities; angels are prepared to set up appointments with them for us. We have often prayed for favour in whole areas. In remarkable ways this has come to pass. We have prayed for angels to visit the areas with visions and dreams prior to our visit, and some of those we encountered have asked us to interpret these dreams, making it apparent that God's angel had been there before us.

Ananias was another person who received a divine appointment. 'But the Lord said to Ananias, "Go! This man is my chosen instrument to carry my name before the Gentiles"' (Acts 9:15). He was not an apostle, prophet or evangelist but a disciple, yet he was told to go to blinded Paul, tell him about Jesus and restore his sight. He overcame his fear and obeyed – with amazing results.

A divine appointment is when God arranges a meeting with a group of people or an individual. It can involve thousands, or it could be one person or your family. Jesus preached and ministered to great crowds. He also took the time and expense to travel great distances to minister to only one person. Those who minister to large crowds need to be open for divine appointments with one person or one family.

God spoke to a Christian lady. His command was clear: go to Australia. After more explicit instructions she arrived there. Three days later she met a man who was an obvious 'set-up' from God. He accepted Christ into his life and was introduced to a good church. The woman was told: 'Now you can go home; you have finished the work I called you here to do.' Do you glimpse the value God places on one human being? All the expense and travelling hours, for just one person's destiny to be secured.

Angels Go Before Us

Rose George, of Crawley, West Sussex, tells of her experience when she went to Uganda with a team from YWAM. She and another person visited some of the homes in one of the villages, taking two interpreters with them. The last home they visited was a family of Muslims.

> We spoke to them about the Lord through our interpreters and the whole family was ready to respond to the gospel and to give their lives to the Lord Jesus. As we were leaving they told us through our interpreters that white people had visited them earlier in the day. I thought some of the team had visited and we had clashed with them. On our return we inquired from the rest of the team to find that nobody had been there. Our team were the only white people in the area. I know that God had sent His angels ahead of us, to prepare the harvest for us.

Doors Open and Waiting

Some time ago I wrote to a leading nursing officer in our town. When I finally met up with this lady, she asked for our help. She had 12 residential homes for the elderly plus six special units for those with learning disabilities. There were 350 residents, of whom 150 received no visits as they did not have any family – they did not even receive a birthday or Christmas card from anyone. They were totally alone except for staff and other residents.

Here was a divine appointment: God had opened a large door of opportunity for us. We are a church of about a thousand people. Our church members are befriending the residents of the old people's homes by visiting and showing love in a number of practical ways. Services have started, and most of the residents love the old hymns and the company of loving, caring people. Scores of people have now been born again in these homes. The nursing officer has a heart for the residents.

Even before this opening, some of the members in our church had worked in some of these residential homes and over the years have seen several hundred people accepting Christ. Some of them are now in heaven.

Another home had a hostile leadership, and it was difficult for us to make any headway until one of the residents called us. He had been attending our church for about three years until ill health and age obliged him to go into this home. He demanded to see one of the church ministers, and after the initial visit requested a service in the home. Five of the residents have received Christ, and our team has started a discipleship group in this home. The initial hostility has been replaced with trust.

There are divine set-ups like this in your sphere of influence, but most of us do not stop to pray and ask God where He is visiting next and where He wants us to go. God will send His angels into the areas where He plans to visit. If we pray and obey, following His creative leadership, doors of opportunity will open for us and our churches.

On one of our missions we were sent to a country which is ruled by an Islamic government. In such countries, sensitivity to the Holy Spirit becomes crucial.

A Chinese friend had asked me to give a present to his sister's husband, who was a Muslim and a high-ranking police officer. After giving the present of a coat, we started talking, exchanging pleasantries. When the man asked me what my job entailed, I was slightly hesitant to begin preaching. Three times he pumped me for information about God. 'Lord,' I said, 'Do you want me to speak to this man about you?'

'Yes,' the Lord replied.

I shared the gospel with him for about 45 minutes. It was an interested man who received my Bible as a gift for future reading. This witness and the gift of a Bible would have been enough to have me deported within 24 hours, but God had set up a divine appointment.

However, the devil will also try to trap us into keeping his appointments. In that same country God was moving powerfully in the schools. Scores of teenagers had been saved, and the devil set a trap for me. A Muslim school teacher approached me, asking for a Bible and seeking to know about the Christian faith. Excitement gripped me and I opened my mouth to preach the gospel. Then a miracle happened: no words came out. Three times I tried, and three times no words came out. After we had left that teacher and the school, Joyce explained to me that the teacher had been trying to get me to witness to him so that he could have reported me to the authorities, and I would have been deported. That had been an appointment set up by the devil. Watch out for them.

Travailing Prayer

Prayer precedes divine appointments. Cornelius and Peter were both praying when God interjected supernatural directives into their 'quiet time'.

The angels have been released to work with us to enable us to reap the harvest, and prayer is the key. 'An angel from heaven appeared to him and strengthened him. And being in anguish, he prayed more earnestly, and his sweat was like drops of blood falling to the ground' (Luke 22:43–4). We may never sweat blood, but all who pray properly will at times travail (as if giving birth) in prayer. Many of us have started a time of prayer in an exhausted state, only to find strength along the way. Watch and pray, lest you enter into temptation. A lack of prayer relates to those who sleep, so awake from sleep and pray. Peter could not keep awake to pray, and later he denied Christ three times. His weak flesh needed to be subdued through prayer. We will receive if we persist. If we pay the price and pray, angels will visit and minister to us and through us. Prayer is a discipline that becomes a delight, but only as we persist in allowing the holy and recreated human Spirit to have the rule of our lives.

How to Release Your Angels to Work on Your Behalf

The Bible is very clear about the constant activity of angels on a believer's behalf, and I want to explain how you can release your angels to work on your behalf at all times. 'For he will command his angels concerning you to guard you in all your ways' (Psalm 91:11). Our Lord is generous, He is not stingy with anything, and He will give His angels. Let us not doubt that. 'But when he asks, he must believe and not doubt, because he who doubts is like a wave of the sea, blown and tossed by the wind. That man should not think he will receive anything from the Lord; he is a double-minded man, unstable in all he does' (James 1:6–8). This is the challenge. When God says that He will give His angels, will you believe it, even though you cannot see them? God will pass over a thousand to get to the one who is believing. God has no favourites; there are only those who believe and those who doubt.

So the first key to releasing your angels is to believe that God will give His angels charge over you. The angels have God's commission to take charge of us. This means they have responsibility to take charge of us personally in every detail. When Satan's demons attack us, the angels are there to deliver us. When we rebuke demons in Jesus' Name, the angels go into action on our behalf. They take charge over us to keep us from danger, death and sickness, in all our ways. Not just some of our ways, but all of them.

Derek Prince, in his book on fasting and prayer, tells how in World War II men always tried to get into his patrol because no one was killed. All returned safely every time. His patrols were the safest place in which to be. Why? As a believer he fasted, prayed and believed God for protection. God gave him and the men with him angels to protect them all from evil.

My wife and I were praying to God for a decent car. Our own Saab had died and we were rattling around in a 'good old runner'. We have been graced with gifts of cars before and we called them our 'faith cars'. This was going to be somewhat different. This new gift was to be known as our 'mercy car'. I will admit we struggled to believe. Neither of us knows much about cars, except where to put the petrol! 'Lord, please give us a reliable, economical car with a sun-roof and a cassette player. Amen,' we prayed. On some ministry trips with the wrong car, you can feel like a wrung-out rag at the end of the journey. Power steering and comfortable seats are a real bonus in a ministry car. In our prayer, Joyce chimed in, 'Lord, a white car, please.'

After months of struggle, the Lord stepped in. A lady came to us and said, 'God has told me to give you this car.' With the keys in our hands we wept tears of joy, knowing that this was not a 'faith car', but a 'mercy car'. It was the best car we have ever been given – four years old, with only 16,000 miles on the clock, reliable, serviced and economical (compared with some old cars that can cost you an arm and a leg to keep going!). It was a gleaming Volvo 440 GLS complete with sun-roof, cassette player, power steering, comfortable seats and – yes, you've guessed it – the colour is white.

I have told this to let you into a trade secret. When the thought flashes into my mind that there might be an accident, I immediately remember that this is the car that God gave us in His mercy, and I say, 'No way, devil! God did not give me this car to die in but to enjoy!' I immediately change the image of destruction into one of victory. I never ask God to go with me on a journey. He said that He will never leave me, and so He is already with me. We do not need to beg God for His angels to protect us. They are charged to keep us in all our ways, including car journeys. When we believe, we receive, and our angels go to work to fulfil God's Word. In their hands they shall bear us up (Psalm 91:12).

Angels Protect Us

In my early flying days, I would picture angels holding the plane's wings up. My wife likes a bit of turbulence – she says the rocking motion helps her to sleep – but I like a smooth flight. So it is hard to get an agreement in prayer from Joyce on this. Some flights, therefore, are smooth and others are turbulent, but always the angels are holding up the wings. 'In their hands they shall bear you up' (Psalm 91:12). Not 'might', but 'shall'. Strong, majestic angels are holding us up. God is so protective and caring we are not even to hurt our feet against any stones. This is the God that I know, the author of life, the life-giving, fun-loving, adventurous, sometimes hilarious Lord who keeps all His children from falling.

We need to renew our thinking. You may be saying, 'Yes, but what about those Christians who died, failed or never got healed?' I say, 'You can be different.' Meditate, think about, soak in that verse from Psalm 91 and other similar verses, and you will not die or be sick before your time, and others will be protected because of your covenant with the Almighty God. 'You will tread upon the lion and the cobra, you will trample the great lion and the serpent' (Psalm 91:13). God has given His angels to keep us safe in their hands, and from that high and lofty place we can tread upon the lion and cobra (demons) because they are under our feet.

Walk in Faith

Some people say they would have liked to have walked with Jesus when He was here on earth. The apostles did this for three years, but Jesus had to rebuke them: 'How foolish you are, and how slow of heart to believe all that the prophets have spoken' (Luke 24:25). The key to believing is not to go on a tour of Israel and walk in the steps of Jesus. The key is to believe the written Word now, today.

When I was reading 'Who redeems your life from the pit and crowns you with love and compassion' (Psalm 103:4), the Lord asked me if I believed it. I gulped! Sometimes we can say, 'Yes, I believe this verse or that scripture,' without the reality of it affecting our daily lives.

I said: 'Lord, I feel a terrible oppression on my head.'

He responded: 'Are they demons, or is the crown upon your head?' My meditation continued on this verse for another 30 minutes, and I made a conscious choice to believe it. Within a short time my head cleared of all oppression.

I was and still am crowned every day with the loving kindness and tender mercies of God. Try reading Psalm 91, stopping at each verse and asking yourself, 'Do I believe this?' If you believe Psalm 91, your present and future are assured. 'I will be with him in trouble; I will deliver him and honour him' (Psalm 91:15). What wonderful promises!

When I first heard about how to walk in faith, Joyce and I began to live in the good of it. On the surface, many others were saying that they were walking by faith, but as I got to know many of these people closely I discovered that they were not in reality living by faith, only speaking as if they were.

Faith versus Doubt

A well-known minister shared with me his battle with doubt. This man was being mightily used by God; he fasted often and rebuked the doubt, but nothing worked for long until the Lord spoke to him on this issue.

The Lord said, 'When you pray and I am answering your prayer, the devil sends a spirit of doubt to overcome your faith. You then often doubt that I've heard you and give up before I can manifest the answer.' It dawned on him that the devil would not waste his time sending the demon of doubt if he did not have faith. With this understanding, when he next prayed and doubt attacked his mind, he lifted his hands and said, 'Thank you, Lord, that the devil has sent the spirit of doubt. Therefore I know I have faith and I know that you have answered my prayer, thereby turning the devil's doubt back on itself.' The devil soon stopped sending doubt to the minister as it only reinforced his faith in God. I tried this: it really worked powerfully.

God has given every believer a measure of faith, and it is clear from the teachings of Jesus that you do not need more than the measure of a mustard seed of faith to move a mountain. Some use their faith to believe their sins are forgiven, while others struggle even to believe that. In my formative early months as a new Christian, thoughts would fill my mind along this line: 'If you were truly a Christian you would never have done that. You are not really a true Christian, are you?' As young Christians many of us experience accusation and condemnation and wonder if we really are Christians after all.

When I used to sin, the recovery period was up to six weeks! The devil tempted. I fell. He then kicked me on the ground and tried to keep me there. In those formative months I fell for his lies, but not now. I am fully persuaded that I am a Christian and my sins are totally forgiven.

The devil tried the same tactics when I used my faith to believe for healing, deliverance, the salvation of others, finances and angelic assistance. The devil comes immediately to try to snatch away the Word of God that is sown into our hearts. How does he do it? With his own seed of doubt: 'Has God said ...?' Even to Jesus the devil said, 'If you are the Son of God ...' We can and we must turn doubt back on itself. When the revelation of God's Word comes, we hold it with a good and noble heart. This is called 'good soil' in the Bible, and produces thirty, sixty or a hundred times from that which has been sown into our hearts.

Believe the Truth

This is the second key: use your measure of faith in God's Word until the revelation is fully established. Persevere and be healed or delivered, or break through in any area that the Word of God covers. For the revelation and understanding of angels to operate successfully in our lives, we have to be fully persuaded that angels are sent by God to minister to the heirs of salvation, to wait upon us. Our attitude must be: 'God said it, I believe it, that settles it!'

Watch What We Speak

The third key to releasing your angels is our 'little member', our tongue. James says that our tongue is little but can often speak the wrong things. Whatever we believe and use our faith for, we must reinforce with our mouths.

The power of life and death is in the tongue. You can die prematurely if your tongue is used for deathly, negative things. We are told to think soberly about our measure of faith, so it does not become presumption. When we work with God's revelation, with heart belief and mouth expression, we can have whatever we say. Let me give a simple example. Some people will say, 'I cannot afford it!' This is based on 'I can't.' While this may be a fact, it may not be the truth. The truth states: 'My God [that's bringing God into the financial need] will supply all my needs according to His riches in Christ Jesus.' The emphasis and focus changes from 'I' to 'Him': 'My God will supply …' I never say I cannot afford it. If God wants me to have it, He will pay for it; and He can afford it!

Be Ready for War

The fourth key is based on the truth of spiritual warfare. We have an enemy who seeks to snatch away the Word of God from our hearts. We must stop him.

'Therefore submit to God. Resist the devil and he will flee from you as in terror' (James 4:7, AMP). 'I tell you the truth, whatever you bind on earth will be bound in heaven, and whatever you loose on earth will be loosed in heaven' (Matthew 18:18).

Angels will go into action when we believe, exercise our measure of faith and line up our tongue (speech) with what is taught in the Word of God.

Walk in Fruitfulness

As we keep the demons away from the seed (revelation), especially about angels, we will walk in great fruitfulness that will bless not only us but the many people our lives touch. God is glorified by us bearing much fruit. Have you now believed the Word of God about angels? Are you using your faith to release your angels' ministry? Are you managing to use your tongue to bring God's life into your revelation? Have you dealt aggressively with the hindrances of the demons? Let us enjoy our adventure with God and discover the truth about God's holy angels.

Deliverance from evil is part and parcel of our ongoing salvation. We are saved, we are being daily saved, and we shall be saved. Relax, and let God take the strain!

God is not boring. I defy those who are bored with their Christian experience to attribute blame to God. It is your fleshly, soulish, bodily desires that are boring. God's ways are exciting ways. He has planned to send out angels to set up divine encounters for us with the godless. Will you take a challenge and do your part to pray? Angels and even more angels will join you as you pray. Your life will never be boring; you will be busy. God's adventures are breathtaking. Don't miss it, be there when God shows up.

Angels and the Harvest

We have entered into a world-wide ingathering of the great harvest. In the Western world we can sometimes be blinkered. Some have made comments that God is not moving in power on the earth, nothing much appears to be happening, but this is only true of where they live. The world is beginning to explode with the gospel.

Larger gospel meetings are being recorded than ever before in some nations. Larger churches have emerged than have ever been seen. A church in Seoul, South Korea, has a membership of one million people. In the UK a good number of churches have grown into thousands. There has been a breakthrough in television. Many of us have prayed for this for more than twenty years. What a glorious happening! The tide has turned. While those in Western Europe are not falling over themselves to get into church, in Eastern Europe the story is different! It will happen here soon too!

Then I saw another angel flying in mid-air, and he had the eternal gospel to proclaim to those who live on the earth – to every nation, tribe, language and people [including Western Europe!]. Then another angel came out of the temple and called in a loud voice to him who was sitting on the cloud, 'Take your sickle and reap, because the time to reap has come, for the harvest of the earth is ripe.' So he who was seated on the cloud swung his sickle over the earth, and the earth was harvested.

Another angel came out of the temple in heaven, and he too had a sharp sickle. Still another angel, who had charge of the fire, came from the altar and called in a loud voice to him who had the sharp sickle, 'Take your sharp sickle and gather the clusters of grapes from the earth's vine, because its grapes are ripe.' The angel swung his sickle on the earth, gathered its grapes and threw them into the great winepress of God's wrath.

(Revelation 14:6, 15–19)

There would appear to be two harvests, reaped in close proximity. The first angel implores Jesus, who is sitting on the cloud, to reap the harvest of the earth, which he does. (He is the head and we are the body, so we, the Church, will do it.) The second angel reaps. First, God's harvest is reaped of those who are saved out of every nation, tribe and tongue. Then follows the harvest of judgement.

> Jesus told them another parable: 'The kingdom of heaven is like a man who sowed good seed in his field. But while everyone was sleeping, his enemy came and sowed weeds among the wheat, and went away. When the wheat sprouted and formed ears, then the weeds also appeared. The owner's servants came to him and said, "Sir, didn't you sow good seed in your field? Where then did the weeds come from?"
>
> '"An enemy did this," he replied.
>
> 'The servants asked him, "Do you want us to go and pull them up?"
>
> '"No," he answered, "because while you are pulling the weeds, you may root up the wheat with them. Let both grow together until the harvest. At that time I will tell the harvesters: First collect the weeds and tie them in bundles to be burned; then gather the wheat and bring it into my barn."'
>
> (Matthew 13:24–30)

There we have it: two harvests, two revivals. One a revival of God, the other a revival of evil from the devil. And the climax is the final great harvest of God being reaped from the earth. When those who are reaped appear at the throne of God, they are taken away from the earth. The ungodly men and women will be reaped for judgement and wrath. Angels are fully involved in both harvests.

Stop Looking Behind: Look Forward

'Surely the day is coming; it will burn like a furnace. All the arrogant and every evildoer will be stubble, and that day that is coming will set them on fire,' says the LORD Almighty. 'Not a root or a branch will be left to them. But for you who revere my name, the sun of righteousness will rise with healing in its wings. And you will go out and leap like calves released from the stall.'

(Malachi 4:1–2)

The Lord is visiting the earth in a powerful way at the time of writing. Reports are coming from all over the world, including the UK, of God 'just showing up'. This is the time of His visitation. He is taking over His Church, and that's revival. More and more doors are opening and the harvest is being gathered in.

Pray as you have never prayed before. Believe and ask for divine appointments. God will honour you and send out His holy angels to help you. This is a new day. Forget the former failures, and even the successes. The reaping, the ingathering, the revival will be unlike anything we have experienced before, and will go beyond our wildest dreams. Move over, devil! Move over, leaders! Move over, believers! God will take over, and we need to prepare ourselves for His awesome visitation.

'Praise be to the Lord, the God of Israel, because he has come and has redeemed his people' (Luke 1:68). When Jesus came to Jerusalem it was their time of visitation, but sadly most of them missed it and Jerusalem was destroyed. Don't miss your time of visitation. God will visit the places where He will call out a people to own His name. 'Live such good lives among the pagans that, though they accuse you of doing wrong, they may see your good deeds and glorify God on the day he visits us' (1 Peter 2:12).

Conclusion

What is from God?

'To another the ability to distinguish between spirits' (1 Corinthians 12: 10). One of the nine gifts of the Holy Spirit is the discerning of spirits. How can you discern if any spiritual experience is genuinely from God?

Recently, in a newspaper article, a young theologian had quotes from her thesis about angels printed. 'Angels appear in similar forms to people of all faiths and are often detected by a sweet smell or a warm sensation.' This young lady claims that angels are not exclusively for Christians, but frequently appear to Hindus, Sikhs, Jews, Muslims and atheists. 'If everyone is seeing the same kind of angels this is very exciting.' She maintains that God will send angels to people of whatever religion, and that non-adherents to any faith in God have been visited by God's angels. The questions raised are these:

- Are these spiritual experiences genuinely from God?
- If people of different religions and those who do not have a faith in God are seeing angels, why is this happening?

As Christians we are commanded to test the spirits, because the Bible warns that the devil can come as an angel of light to deceive. 'Dear friends, do not believe every spirit, but test the spirits to see whether they are from God' (1 John 4:1). Therefore, if each experience needs to be tested, the conclusion is that every spiritual experience is not necessarily God's doing. There are wicked spirits out there who also will give 'nice' spiritual experiences.

Here are five ways by which we test the spirits.

- Does what they are doing or saying line up with God's authority, the Word of God? A man of God who has seen angels on numerous occasions said, 'God and I have an understanding: everything shared must be confirmed by two or three witnesses [scriptures] from the Bible.' God didn't mind this man's approach. Let's make it ours!
- Does the experience take us to God or to other things? In other words, do you love and worship God more than before that experience? The Bible is very clear: worship is reserved for Jesus Christ only. If there is any worship of angels, of a human being or any other gods, your experience is a false one. It is not from God.
- Do you have the witness of the Holy Spirit, a witness of peace?
- Have you become more or less obedient to the Lord Jesus since the encounter?
- Are you willing to submit this experience to your leadership? If you are a leader, even the main leader, are you willing to submit this experience to other leaders for wise counsel or corporate discernment? Are you teachable even if a correction is involved?

A family was receiving regular visits from what they considered to be an angel. My test of this spirit revealed it was not an angel of God. This lady refused the counsel I gave her. She died some years later in a very mysterious way at a young age.

God's Love

The reason God's angels will visit and help people who are with or without religion is because of His great love for all people. This does not mean that their beliefs and lifestyle have earned it – it is usually quite the opposite. A loving God will despatch His holy hand-picked angels to deliver or help an afflicted or endangered person. God's purpose is to draw that human being into His love, not only to know and experience God's love, but to be continually knowing that God of love.

Not for Fun!

If you chase angels for experiences, the demonic powers will accommodate you. You will be deceived and led astray, with often disastrous consequences. Be cautioned against the phenomena of angelic memorabilia, and against long conversations with angels. Our focus must be the Lord Jesus Christ. In His wisdom He will give us experiences as and when He sees it is necessary. 'But seek first his kingdom and his righteousness, and all these things will be given to you as well' (Matthew 6:33). Stay with God. Don't look for the sensational, but stay focused on Him and serve Him with or without supernatural angelic experiences. That is the true call of a disciple. 'Come and learn from me,' said Jesus.

Not Beggars

If you have ever begged God for the gifts of the Holy Spirit, please stop now! The gifts are in the Holy Spirit, and the Holy Spirit lives in you. That should bring you peace.

I have brought literally hundreds of people through to speaking in tongues by asking these questions: Did you pray for God to baptize you in the Holy Spirit? Did you ask God for the gifts of the Holy Spirit? Most seekers will affirm that they have asked for this on numerous occasions. So how do you know you are not baptized with the Holy Spirit? 'Because I do not speak in tongues' is the most common reply. Why don't you stop asking and start to thank God for the baptism you have received? Why don't you thank God for the gift of tongues?

This is based on the scriptures. How much more will the heavenly Father give the Holy Spirit to those who ask. When we are in the realm of faith, not begging, it is very easy to flow with speaking in tongues. It is no different in the operation of the other gifts. If we think that we don't have something, we beg God for it. We then become tense. The way we operate in the gifts is by being relaxed, not by being tense. When we ask our heavenly Father for this experience, we must do our part to believe that God has heard our prayer and is now answering us. One seeker came and said, 'This won't take long. I've asked, now I'm receiving.' Within minutes that seeker was filled and flowing in the gifts.

Discernment

What is discernment of spirits? Discernment of spirits is discerning spirits. Simple, isn't it? Discernment of human spirits, discernment of the Holy Spirit, discernment of angelic spirits (that is why many have perceived angels although never seeing them). We can also discern demon spirits. Probably everyone has perceived demon spirits at some point or another. When we walk through certain areas of town, what do we discern? When someone gives a prophecy in church and it is from God, we can discern the presence of the Holy Spirit. We can discern the operation of the Holy Spirit. When we have heard a prophecy that was not from the Holy Spirit, we may have thought it sounded right but that something was not quite fitting. How many of us have experienced that? We often discern the human spirit and motivation in operation. How many of us have discerned when the Holy Spirit is in operation and we knew He was around? How many of us have discerned that a prophecy was wrong?

We say we don't want to judge that brother or sister, but we are told to judge prophecy. How many of us have discerned an evil spirit? It is important that we allow this gift to flow. This is one of the major ways that you can discern whether it is an angel sent by God or a demonic spirit. The Bible says that the devil comes as an angel of light to deceive. This is especially true with the New Age movement, but we can discern. How many of us heard a teaching and deep down inside it didn't sit right? Well, we do have gifts, then. We don't have to beg God for what we already have.

We can flow and relax because we are in faith. Faith is a wonderful key. The working of miracles is a gift from God that people put out of reach. They leave it for the spiritual ones, but the working of miracles is a gift. I have seen young Christians in the Philippines running up and down the mountains commanding cripples and the dead to rise up because they saw their pastors do it. They copied them. Their lives were not all sorted out. Gifts are not to do with maturity – gifts are gifts. We have the discernment of spirits: that means the other gifts are in there as well, waiting to come out.

Scepticism, rationalism, unbelief have put the working of miracles out of reach. We have to be like children, saying, 'Thank you, Lord, for giving me these gifts. I am going to release them by believing.' We can and do discern human spirits. My wife once said to me, 'Don't leave me alone with that man. I don't know what, but there is something wrong there.'

I said, 'You have to love him, he is our brother in Christ – you can't think like that.' He raped a girl six weeks later! My wife discerned a human spirit and motive; so can all of us.

This wonderful gift is not to be confused with the gift of suspicion, though. As we read earlier, 'Dear friends, do not believe every spirit, but test the spirits to see whether they are from God' (1 John 4:1). Even if we see a wonderful angel in magnificent light who appears to us, we are still supposed to test that vision or revelation.

Test Everything

When thoughts come into our minds, we are to test them. Some act as though every thought is from God. This is not true. We are clearly instructed to test the spirits. Revelations or thoughts that bully or push us are not from God. The Good Shepherd leads us. Our peace is our umpire. If there is an absence of peace, put a big question-mark against that experience. In other words, we can test the angels and prophecy. We are told to test them: we don't swallow everything that comes our way, or believe every voice or spirit. Very often, when there is an evil spirit involved, if you test it, it begins to turn into what it really is: nasty, pushy and bullying. The devil is a tyrant. We can discern evil and rebuke it, even if it comes in a mushy way.

When I was a young Christian there was a lady in a church who was giving prophecies. They sounded good, but when we shared about it later on, every one of us thought that although these prophecies sounded right on the surface they were not quite right. She was saying, 'My children, I love you,' and things like that. A visiting speaker came by; right in the meeting he pointed at her and said, 'In the Name of Jesus, spirit of divination, come out of her.' She screamed, fell down and rolled; the spirit came out of her. Afterwards we all knew, really. It's incredible: we had the discernment, but sometimes – and this is a seed I want to leave you with – we push our discernment down and conclude we must not think like that about that brother or that sister. Discernment of spirits is given by God for a purpose: it is to warn us, so we can know what to do in a given situation. With this discernment we can understand what is happening in the spiritual realm.

Worship God Only

'At this I fell at his feet to worship him. But he said to me, "Do not do it! I am a fellow-servant with you and with your brothers who hold to the testimony of Jesus. Worship God! For the testimony of Jesus is the spirit of prophecy" ' (Revelation 19:10). The angel was saying to John, 'You must not worship me. You must worship God.' We are commanded by God Himself not to worship angels. Any angel that seeks or demands worship is not sent by God.

We must not be afraid. Many people get scared of the supernatural realm. They get scared of angels because somebody had a flaky experience and they heard about it. When someone misuses the gifts, the answer is not to stop using God's gifts. If we throw the baby out with the bath water, we also throw the truth out.

We embrace truth, but throw out the extremes. Do not be tempted to hold long conversations with angels: let's have long conversations with Jesus. Some of us need to believe in a new way, to allow angels to come and do what they need to do with us and through us. Every time we go into ministry they are actively involved with us. Every time we open our mouths and speak to somebody about Jesus, they are actively involved with us. Every time we go into that job situation they are there to bring favour and promotion, to do the will of the Lord. They are in our situation for a purpose, for us to fulfil the will of God.

Know God's Will

Let me tell you, depression, heaviness, poverty, struggling all the time – these do not fulfil the will of God. The angels are sent so that we can succeed and begin to rise up and see these negatives broken. Then we will demonstrate the kingdom of God, when we proclaim the kingdom of God to our neighbours and they can see we are a highly favoured people. We are someone who is set apart. Angels were sent to prepare the ground before people went into a situation. God said, 'I am going to send the angel before your face, into situations to prepare the way for you.' You are a witness for Christ. Can you see this? Angels going ahead of us to set everything in order? When we arrive, things have already been prepared. Our heavenly Father has not withheld His own Son from us: will He not freely give us all things (including angelic involvement) to reach and fulfil our destiny in God?

Let us speak the words that release our angels. They do the bidding of the Word of God. When we confess and believe the Word of God, the angels go into action. We are to enjoy God's provision. We are to enter into the rest of faith. We are to possess our godly inheritance. In these dangerous and often precarious times, people need a fresh revelation about angels. This will help release thousands from fear to faith and freedom. God has sent His angelic hosts to help us frail human beings. It is the time for us to know of their existence, function and purpose, to learn how to work together with the angels to gather in the last, greatest harvest before the return of our Lord Jesus Christ.

MARANATHA – COME SOON, LORD JESUS.